"Healing Well and Living F  is a
practical and spiritual guide ll of
recovery applications for h ned
therapist and survivor who : for
a journey worth pursuing."

Sandra L. Brown, MA, The Institute for Relational Harm
Reduction & Public Pathology Education;
author of *How to Spot a Dangerous Man Before
You Get Involved* and *Women Who Love Psychopaths*

"This book provides authentic hope and lasting healing for individuals and families who have been traumatized from the effects of an abusive relationship. Dr. Ramona's personal story of healing well from an abusive relationship is compelling and provides biblical wisdom, practical instruction, and hope-focused counsel for those who have remained silent in their suffering. Dr. Ramona saturates the content with her gentle and empathetic approach to overcoming the collateral damage emotionally, relationally, and spiritually to these life shattering issues."

Dr. Tim Clinton, president of the
American Association of Christian Counselors

"This book [is] relevant, uplifting, and certainly one-of-a-kind. The profound nature of *Healing Well and Living Free* offers readers an opportunity to personally connect with Dr. Ramona's story of her own transformation, as well as providing concrete steps surrounding how it is that we are able to step into freedom. A mustread for those who have been victimized, as well as for those of us who love someone who has . . . which ultimately means everyone."

Jessica Yaffa, domestic violence overcomer; founder of
No Silence No Violence; author; speaker; advocate

"Healing Well and Living Free from an Abusive Relationship is an important and brave book for anyone who has experienced

the secret shame of domestic abuse. Dr. Ramona is not only an expert in helping a victim heal but has also been a victim herself, which makes her words all the more compelling and credible. Safety is not the end goal but healing the damage and eventually thriving is. Dr. Ramona's book shows the way and gives the tools to get there."

Leslie Vernick, speaker; relationship coach; author of seven books, including the bestselling *The Emotionally Destructive Relationship* and *The Emotionally Destructive Marriage*

"*Healing Well and Living Free* is a practical gift of sharing and encouragement for those who are seeking a path of hope and healing. Dr. Ramona provides that path by detailing the three personal stages—Victim, Survivor, and Overcomer—in the journey out of domestic abuse to really living and loving free. . . . Dr. Ramona is a former military spouse, a certified Domestic Violence Counselor with a Doctorate in Psychology, a strong person of faith, and . . . a domestic violence abuse Overcomer herself, . . . and her writing exudes the wisdom, confidence, authority, and sensitivity from her qualifications."

James H. Mukoyama Jr., major general, US Army-Retired; president and CEO of Military Outreach USA

"*Healing Well and Living Free from an Abusive Relationship* is timely and on target. Dr. Ramona has come up with solutions that offer simple and clear guidelines that are easy to understand. She is a survivor who has overcome twenty years of domestic violence with firsthand knowledge of how dangerous and frightening the life of the abused spouse is. I am delighted that at last domestic violence and abuse in relationships can be systematically and squarely addressed in simple ways that are easy to follow and understand."

Her Excellency Dr. Inonge Mbikusita-Lewanika, Zambian ambassador to the United States and European Union

"As a retired NFL player with the San Diego Chargers and a pastor of Rock Church San Diego . . . , I am fully aware that domestic violence takes place both off the field and away from the pew. Dr. Ramona's story confirms that this can happen to anyone, and proves that healing well and living free is possible for those who pursue it. Her personal story of overcoming the aftermath of domestic violence will inspire you and provide you with the steps to take in your own healing-well journey."

Miles McPherson, pastor, Rock Church, San Diego;
author; retired NFL player

"I have known Dr. Ramona for over thirty years, and this work reflects her heart of compassion, academic rigor, spiritual insight, and counseling competence. . . . Dealing with the symptoms of an abusive relationship and not the sources results in short-term gain and long-term pain, which tends to reinforce the cycle of despair. This book does not promise easy answers that are not likely to last the test of time. The good news is that it radiates with contagious hope, spiritual wisdom, experienced insight, and practical help. Do you want to heal well and live free? I suggest that you carefully, patiently, and enthusiastically embrace these life lessons and integrate them into your own real-time and real-world experiences."

Ken Nichols, PsyD, founder and executive director
of ALIVE Ministries; author

"*Healing Well and Living Free from an Abusive Relationship* . . . clearly lays out the steps to authentically heal well from the aftermath of domestic violence. . . . I have rarely, if ever, so profited from reading a book as I have this superb . . . presentation. Dr. Ramona's transparency and empathy will encourage you to believe that you too can heal well and live free!"

Dr. John Edmund Haggai, founder of
Haggai International; author

"Dr. Ramona has written a beautifully moving and compelling account of her journey from the suffering of abuse to the wholeness and freedom of healing. . . . Her story—and the answers she discovered—will inspire and help all who read it."

Rev. Jack Wyman, retired pastor; state lawmaker; candidate for governor and US Senate

Healing Well and Living Free
from an Abusive Relationship

Healing Well

and

Living Free

from an Abusive

Relationship

From Victim to Survivor
to Overcomer

Dr. Ramona Probasco

a division of Baker Publishing Group
Grand Rapids, Michigan

375 0272

Published by Revell
a division of Baker Publishing Group
PO Box 6287, Grand Rapids, MI 49516-6287
www.revellbooks.com

Printed in the United States of America

Library of Congress Cataloging-in-Publication Data
Names: Probasco, Ramona, 1967– author.
Title: Healing well and living free from an abusive relationship : from victim to survivor to overcomer / Dr. Ramona Probasco.
Description: Grand Rapids : Baker Publishing Group, 2018. | Includes bibliographical references and index.
Identifiers: LCCN 2017057406 | ISBN 9780800729653 (pbk. : alk. paper)
Subjects: LCSH: Abused women. | Abusive men. | Psychotherapy.
Classification: LCC HV6626 .P745 2018 | DDC 362.82/9286—dc23
LC record available at https://lccn.loc.gov/2017057406

Events in this book are described to the best of the author's recollection. In some cases the names and details of the people and situations described have been changed or presented in composite form in order to ensure the privacy of those with whom the author has worked.

18 19 20 21 22 23 24   7 6 5 4 3 2 1

To my precious children . . .
No one gets to choose their childhood, but we all get to choose our response to it. Growing up, you each found yourself on a path that offered plenty of excuses for you to give up, to compromise, or to blame. Yet none of you have done this. Overcomers do not deny their past or their pain. Rather, they choose to heal from it, learn from it, and share with others who desire to listen. Each of you, in your own way, is doing this. You are the impetus behind my decision to heal well and live free. This choice, inspired by your love and grace, has changed my life forever. We are overcomers. We are free!
I love you dearly, Mama

To you, the reader . . .
Your courage and commitment to healing well and living free is one of the greatest gifts you can choose to give yourself. It begins with a decision that only you can make. It results in an outcome that will impact your life in ways unforeseen at this point. What I can assure you is that you will not walk this course alone. I will lay out every step along the way and pray for strength to carry you onward. You are much stronger than you realize. You are worth every bit of effort this will require. You deserve everything healing well will bring. You deserve to be free!

Contents

Contents

Foreword

This issue of domestic violence has been something that has been glossed over, set aside, and quite honestly ignored for years. I ask myself why . . . is it because in our male-dominated world it is not an issue that in large part directly affects us as men? I am aware that violence behind closed doors happens to both men and women. Statistically, however, women are disproportionately more likely to be victimized by a male, treated as an object, exploited, and abused. Regardless of one's gender, it is a crime and a travesty that mandates our collective attention as a society and as individuals. We must no longer look the other way.

This issue has infiltrated all socioeconomic, ethnic, cultural, and religious groups. Therefore, domestic violence affects all of us either directly or indirectly. Since one in four women in the United States will be a victim of domestic violence at some point in her life, all of us either know someone who is caught in the perils of this evil, or we ourselves have been or are experiencing trauma of this nature.

It is only now in the area of social media, and with the help of the enormous platform that is the National Football League, that these deplorable incidences have been and are being played out before us nationally. Domestic violence is a conversation and a concern that is now easily a top-five hot button issue that needs to be addressed in our society. As a man and a former NFL player I am saddened by the conduct of my peers and my younger, current contemporaries; and as a husband of over twenty years and a father of three daughters I cannot accept where things currently stand. My heart breaks for the children who grow up hearing and seeing this horror. How can a child grow up unscathed when he or she witnessed abuse in their home? The answer is . . . they can't.

This is why I lend my name and support behind Dr. Ramona Probasco. To me she is a picture of courage, willing to be vulnerable and transparent through her own painful past in an effort to lift others out of their current dark reality. I firmly believe the tools, training, resources, and experience she provides in this space is a part of the solution our society needs to move the needle in a more positive direction.

Ray McElroy,
former NFL player and Chicago Bears chaplain;
author; speaker; CEO of A Ray of Hope on Earth
non-profit organization; co-owner of R.M.M.
Renovation and Restoration LLC

Preface

Until you call it what it is, you're going to call it what it's not.

Dr. Ramona

For many years in my marriage, I did everything I could to try to save it. To me, promises are sacred. When I said, "I do," it meant forever. I come from a long lineage of never-say-die stalwarts. And in many situations, this is an admirable trait. But in an abusive marriage, it can be a deadly one. Like many who experience abuse from their intimate partner, I called it everything but that.

Abusers were those scary-looking people in prison mug shots whose cold, blank stares send a chill down your spine. And victims were those weak, indecisive, afraid-of-their-own-shadow kind of people who didn't know how to stand up for themselves. So when I married my tall, dark, and handsome heartthrob (and I'm not embellishing a bit here), I practically levitated as I walked down the aisle. The thought that three years later he'd pick me up like a rag doll and throw me against the headboard of our bed was as inconceivable to me as splitting an atom with a butter knife. No way, not me. Not him. Not us.

What I didn't realize is that my experience was textbook in many ways. I minimized the verbal, emotional, and physical assaults, calling them everything and anything but abuse. I was not a victim, and he was not an abuser. I truly believed I could love him into wellness. But until you call it what it is, you're going to call it what it's not. I did just that. If you're anything remotely like me, you may be doing the same thing, saying things like, "We have a communication problem," "We need to learn how to resolve conflict better," or "We're just going through a stressful time." These are just a few of the erroneous phrases I used to minimize the abuse I was enduring—and ones I commonly hear when working with clients who have experienced abuse from their intimate partners.

I don't intend to advise you on whether or not to remain in your relationship. You alone can decide that. This book is actually the by-product of years spent pursuing authentic healing in my own life. As I began to notice seedlings of a new and healthier life growing in me, I started to share what I was learning with others struggling as I once did. As months turned into years, I began teaching graduate students what I had learned and what I had found to work in my life. I was then invited to speak on the subject matter. After all this, I was still shocked when one of my workshop attendees asked where they could purchase my book!

This book is my story—my story of how I got into, through, and out of an abusive marriage. At the same time, it's more than that. In a very personal, straightforward, honest sort of way, I pull back the curtain and let you see the secrets I held, the battle I fought, and the surrender that inevitably saved me from myself. Abusive relationships can leave emotional scars that seem inconceivable to truly heal from. What I discovered is that we can heal—and not just heal but heal well. Healing well is the precursor to living free. As a woman of deep faith, I believe we were created for freedom. Abuse in marriage is the kryptonite to freedom. Abuse, regardless of how it manifests itself, will destroy the trust and, in the end, can destroy the relationship. More importantly, it can destroy you, and you matter.

The comforting news is . . . you can heal. You can make intentional decisions and take one step at a time to move forward and not merely move on. My heartfelt desire is that you will allow me to come alongside you as you courageously take each step. With your permission, I'd like to be a sort of sojourner supporting you and encouraging you in your journey.

What I can promise you is there is life, a great life, awaiting you. There is life after abuse. But to heal well and live free, you must choose to do so. It won't just happen. It will take effort and commitment on your part. It will be, perhaps, the hardest endeavor you have ever achieved.

This is not going to be a casual, poolside read. I have included questions at the end of each chapter that I encourage you to thoughtfully answer at your own pace. Please consider working with a counselor who has an accurate, truth-based understanding of abuse in the context of an intimate relationship. Abuse isolates us from others. One of the greatest gifts you can give yourself is to connect with trustworthy people who can support you as you work through this book.

I understand that not everyone who reads this book may embrace faith in God. My desire is not to talk you into believing in God. Issues of this nature are matters we all get to decide. I simply share my story and how having an accurate understanding that I am fully loved and accepted was a huge catalyst to deep healing in me personally. I'm not here to pressure you. I'm merely here to love you where you're at. No more, no less.

I recognize and fully acknowledge that abuse takes place in all sorts of relationships. My heart breaks for all victims. However, because the majority of abuse is perpetrated by a male toward a female, I have utilized the pronouns *he* to represent an abuser and *she* to represent a victim. This is not meant to disregard the pain experienced in other contexts; it is merely a way to communicate with clarity. Domestic violence is also commonly referred to as intimate partner violence, and it is broadly defined to include all acts of physical, sexual, psychological, or economic violence that may be committed by a family member or intimate partner. You will notice that I use these terms interchangeably.

I'm so proud of you for considering the pursuit of healing well and living free in your own life. You will never regret your decision. You are meant to live, *really* live, and to love, *really* love.

Now I'll begin with one particular day in my story when I could no longer call it what it's not . . .

Introduction

Something Broke Inside Me

"I can't do it this time," I said. "I can't come back."
"Why not?" he asked.
"Because this time is different. This time something broke inside me."

These are the words I exchanged with my former husband shortly after one of his most ferocious physical assaults. What started as what, for some couples, might be a typical husband-and-wife disagreement had escalated into something dark and ugly.

Ben—his name has been changed for privacy purposes—and I were scheduled to attend a business meeting. I was almost finished dressing, but Ben was still stretched out on the bed.

"When are you going to get ready?" I asked. "People are counting on us."

He offered no response.

This was not a new argument for us. Ben would often back out of commitments at the last possible minute, while I always tried to keep my promises. As the minutes ticked by, I struggled to remain calm, but my stomach was in knots.

"We've got to go. You have to get ready," I said, my anxiety intensifying. I could tell this wasn't going well, and I knew the pattern. We could be headed for a family outing to Disneyland or to an event at which we were the featured speakers. At the last possible minute, Ben would stall, change his mind, and back out. Or at least lead me to believe he might back out. It was exhausting.

Ben's temper was unpredictable. Sometimes he could be persuaded. Other times he would fly into a rage if I questioned him. His emotions could escalate quickly, going from zero to one hundred in a matter of seconds. I never knew if it was safe for us to discuss things or to disagree, and this not knowing kept me on edge.

That particular night our bickering continued as I finished my makeup. When our argument hit its peak, he cornered me in the bathroom while I was sitting on the toilet. By the time I saw the darkening anger in his eyes, I had no way to escape.

Ben is a big man, 6′2″ and 250 pounds. When he is angry, his jaw clenches, and he puffs out his chest. It is almost like seeing one of those sharks on the Discovery Channel circling its prey before it attacks.

As he approached me, his face contorted in anger. I was trapped. Ben lunged at me and grabbed my head in his hands, driving his thumbs into my eye sockets. I couldn't move, couldn't get up. I remember thinking my skull might crack. I feared my head might split open from the enormous force. The pain was excruciating.

As I struggled under his grip, his thumbs dug even deeper into my eyes. To this day, when I close my eyes, I can remember the horrible feeling of his thumbs rolling around in my eye sockets. I could not escape. He had me cornered. I just wanted it to be over. That was the last thing I remember.

After Ben left the bathroom, my youngest daughter, age eleven at the time, came running in. I'd just stumbled into the shower, trying to "wash away" what had happened. I remember my daughter crying and pleading, "Just leave him!" She was desperate. "You can do it, Mom! We can do it together!"

This was a horrific moment for her and for me. It affected me emotionally and physically. I could tell that something was terribly wrong with my vision. For the next several days, everything I saw was blurry. The sides of my skull throbbed, as did my eye sockets. I was petrified that my vision would never recover.

Thank God it did. But something happened that day that would change my life forever. At the precise moment when my physical ability to see was impaired, my internal ability to see came into focus.

Something broke inside me. My nearly twenty-year fight to make our marriage work was gone, and the pain I felt inside for my kids was unbearable. Mentally, emotionally, and physically, I was totally depleted. But at the same time, I could no longer silence my own voice.

I might not have realized it then, but a couple days later when I finally told him, "I can't do it this time; I can't (emotionally) come back," I took my first step toward freedom. All the years of trying to "save the marriage" and "love him into wellness" had brought me to one unmistakable conclusion: it was time to save myself. It was time to love myself enough to believe that trying harder was no longer an option and that he was never going to change. On that day, with bruises still marking my face and neck, I made my first step toward healing well and living free. I chose me.

This is my story. And you might ask, "How can you go from being tossed like a rag doll to writing a book about healing from domestic abuse?" To be completely honest, the fact that I'm here now writing my story is shocking even to me!

Today I am whole again. I have learned to listen to my own voice and to honor and respect myself. I am free from an unhealthy, abusive marriage. My children are safe. I am happily remarried. I have a thriving counseling practice where I've been able to hear hundreds of women's stories and help them along the path to healing from an abusive relationship. I even get to travel the country, telling my story and speaking about healing well from domestic violence. There is hope for you too. I am living proof of it. In the pages that follow, I'll walk you through the actual steps I took to free myself from this relationship not only physically but also emotionally. I will teach you what I teach others who desire to heal well from the trauma that an abusive relationship causes. There is no quick fix. There are no easy answers. But there is a path to healing that you can take one step at a time.

You can heal. It will not be an easy road, but this one thing I can guarantee: where it takes you will be far better than the destination of the road you were on. Trust me. It all starts with the first step. We'll walk together. You can do this.

You may not believe that things will ever change, that your life can ever be different. But for now, know that I believe in you. And in time, you can learn to believe in yourself.

Until then, *believe in my belief.*

1

My Story

After greeting Amber, I sat in the comfortable brown leather chair in my office and invited her to sit down as well. Amber sat down warily, holding a fresh cup of hot tea. She wore workout clothes, and her brown hair was pulled back into a ponytail she'd tucked under a ball cap. She sipped her tea. After a few moments of quiet, I smiled at her, and she weakly smiled back.

Sensing her anxiety, I wanted to set Amber at ease by affirming her decision to pursue counseling. I let her know that I understood how difficult it can be to open up to a person you've never met before. Over the next few minutes, as I gently asked her questions, she began to share her story with me. It wasn't long before her tears began to flow.

You see, Amber hadn't told her story to anyone yet. And as she began to speak, I felt empathy and something else. A rising hope. Why? Because that first step—telling your story—is absolutely necessary for healing from an abusive relationship. I've been blessed to see this process hundreds of times now in my career.

Authentic healing from an abusive relationship begins with telling your story. When you tell your story, even to yourself, you're taking an honest inventory of where you are, how you have changed, and how living a secret life behind closed doors has altered you.

Your story belongs to you, and it's yours to tell. It is no one else's. It is yours alone. Telling your story will give you power over it and eventually allow you to make peace with it.

I'll go first.

You have heard about the turning point—the moment I realized something had to change. Now come with me as we turn back the hands of time so you can take a brief glimpse into the years that led up to that horrific day—the day I experienced one of the most frightening physical assaults by my former husband and the day I finally realized that I could no longer save my marriage.

While my story involves many broken promises, broken dreams, and a broken heart, it did not begin that way.

Once upon a Time

My growing-up years were wonderful in many ways. I am the oldest of three children, with two younger brothers. My parents came from very different backgrounds. My father escaped from a communist country when he was still a teenager, and my mother was raised in the Midwest by a saint of a mother but a tyrant of a father. My parents were and are overcomers, strong and resilient with hearts of gold.

While my family was loving and traditional, much of my childhood was riddled with seasons of financial instability. By the time I was seventeen years old, we had moved numerous times. My dad was a land developer with a keen eye for real estate. He built beautiful custom homes and magnificent subdivisions. I am proud of my dad in many ways. Even so, his tenacity to never give up was both a blessing and a curse. Knowing when to surrender was not his strong point. His willingness to take risks was an asset when he ran for his life across the communist border, but this same trait at times cost him and his family dearly. I can see in my own life how this has been something I, too, have struggled with and have had to learn how to manage in a healthier way.

The industry my dad chose provided the opportunity for big rewards but also the potential for big risks. In this environment, his relentless work ethic and never-say-die attitude paid off tremendously, and we enjoyed luxuries that others could not. But at the same time, the risks caused my family and my mom a great deal of pain. As an adult, I understand the risks, but as a child, they were troubling. One year my dad would be named "Builder of the Year," and the next, due to a downturn in the economy, he would lose everything. We never knew when the other shoe was going to drop. I remember coming home from school one day to find a man repossessing my mother's Cadillac from the garage. Throughout it all, my mom showed a quiet strength that was the backbone of our family. I now realize that she passed this characteristic on to me. For that, I am so thankful.

During the summer between my sophomore and junior years of high school, we spent a couple months in California while my father explored the area for potential business endeavors. On that summer vacation to the Pacific Coast, my life took a significant turn. At age sixteen, I met my future husband, Ben, in a perfect, teenage romantic, storybook moment. Ironically, it was my father who introduced us. I say "ironically" because my parents kept me pretty sheltered. Since I was the only girl, my parents were very protective, sending me to an all-girls private school. I had never really dated or even had opportunities to meet boys before I met Ben.

My Prince

One afternoon I went for a walk on the beach with a friend. When I came back, Ben was there, kicking a soccer ball around with my brothers. By the time I arrived, Ben had met my parents. My dad introduced me to this tall, handsome boy, a sophomore in college with six-pack abs. He said, "I'd like for you to meet my daughter, Ramona." I was immediately drawn to him. Ben had a sharp wit and goofy, boyish appeal.

We went on our first date before my family left California to return home. Ben was the perfect gentleman and even brought me a dozen roses. My parents let us take their car, and he took me out to dinner on a ferryboat on the water. He had a great sense of humor, and I remember a lot of laughing.

After that summer vacation, my dad announced that we would be moving to the West Coast. While I was upset to leave my friends, I was excited to reunite with Ben. He'd been calling me almost every day since our date, and our romance had gained momentum.

The next few years were rocky ones for both me and my family. But whenever I found myself overwhelmed by my circumstances, Ben was my knight in shining armor. He would give me a ride, bring groceries, or simply offer a shoulder to cry on. He became my own personal hero.

It seemed to me that Ben always put me first. I remember how I used to watch his college soccer games on television. One night during a particularly difficult time for my family, I was planning to watch his game on TV. The sportscasters were announcing the players as they ran onto the field, but when they announced Ben's name, he wasn't there. This puzzled me. Shortly afterward, there was a knock on my door, and there he was. He had left the game to be by my side instead. Ben grew to mean more and more to me in many ways.

During that time, I came to understand Jesus in a new and personal way. In fact, Ben was the first one to talk to me about Him. Early in our relationship, he asked me what I thought about Jesus. I remember thinking, *Wow, is he a Jesus freak?* But it was through Ben and a few dear friends that my relationship with God deepened and became a stabilizing force in my life.

Ben and I continued to date, most of the time from a distance. When Ben was a sophomore in college, he left school to join the military. He spent the next four years in a special operations division. He became obsessed with training, toughness, and being at the top of his class. He broke battalion records and would repeat the mantra he had been taught: "Kill, kill, kill." I saw him slowly transform before my eyes, but I continued to trust him.

Throughout those tumultuous end-of-high-school years, Ben romanced me from afar, solidifying what I thought was genuine attachment. Ours was a storybook romance. My girlfriends would gather to hear his love letters. He would send me FTD bouquets, and my friends would swoon.

During my freshman year of college, Ben proposed. I was taken aback. After all, he was the only man I'd ever dated, and I knew I was still young. While I was very hesitant, I said, "If you promise to support me through my highest degree, then I'll go for it with you." He agreed.

By this time, I was starting to see signs of trouble in our relationship, but even early on, I ignored my gut. One minute Ben could be charming, and the next moment I would see another side of him. Often I would mail him care packages. In one of them, I included a photo album. A particular photo set Ben off. It was of me and a bunch of college friends, including some guy friends. Upset by this, he drove all through the night from Georgia to my college in Tulsa, Oklahoma. When my phone rang, he said he was waiting downstairs in my dorm. "I came to see you," he said.

Ben was furious about one of the guys in the photo, assuming I had been romantically involved with him in some way. He said he had driven all night, across country, to beat up my friend. I managed to calm him down and told him that everything he was thinking was simply not true. Later that night, he agreed to meet my friend. When he did, he saw for himself that my friend was a nice person. Ben even asked for his forgiveness.

Now I know that his quick turnaround was odd, but at the time, I decided, "Okay, he must really care about me." While Ben's reaction scared me, I minimized it in my mind. I convinced myself that he loved me, and I chose to focus on his good side.

Looking back, most of the times with Ben were wonderful. When we were able to be together, I was swept off my feet. We attended romantic military balls in formal attire. We rode roller coasters until our heads spun. He treated me to four-course fancy dinners. We had a special rock, "our rock," where we watched the sun set over the ocean. Ben even drew a sketch of us sitting there together that I framed.

To me, Ben was romantic, attentive, caring, and supportive. I felt loved, and I was falling for him, hard. We dated for three and a half years before marrying. What I didn't realize at the time was that our brief rendezvous were definitely not the ideal way to really get to know someone. We were separated by miles, and our limited exposure allowed him to maintain a perfect façade that would eventually begin to crumble after we wed.

Just prior to our wedding, I began to see more problems. He would call me names or put me down, saying things to cause me to doubt myself. If I expressed any discontent or concern about our pending marriage, he would explode. I remember him saying multiple times, "Just give me the ring then. It's over!" But those negative moments were followed by wonderful ones. One minute he could be harsh, but the next minute he could be playful and attentive.

Why didn't I run for the hills? I just didn't. The way I saw it, Ben had always been there for me when I needed someone. It seemed to me that the distance and time spent apart were emotionally hard on both of us. Marriage appeared to be the perfect solution. So Ben and I stood at the altar, marrying at the ripe old ages of nineteen and twenty-two years old.

Thus begins my story of falling in love, marrying, and having three incredible children, all while growing up and then growing apart. Unfortunately, what began like a fairy tale romance would turn out to be anything but blissful. Tragedy would soon unfold in my life, and the starry-eyed teenager would become the black-eyed wife.

In the following chapters, I will continue my story of love, marriage, children, and abuse. I will attempt to tell you the whole story—the moments I am proud of and the moments I would just as soon forget.

Through It All

I believe that God protected me and my children through all those years. When I was walking through the darkest days, I felt the Lord saying to me, "I am with you, even when you don't feel Me." He is the One who ultimately helped me turn my focus away from saving my marriage and believing that I could love Ben into wellness. God never stopped showing me how much He loved me and how He desired that I live in freedom. He gave me the tenacity to survive and move forward with resilience.

Today I can say with assurance that God is good. God loves me. He continues to walk with me through my story. He is healing my children and me day by day, and He desires to do the same for you.

No matter how despicable or desperate your situation might be, I am convinced there is hope for you too. And I believe that God can use these experiences to bring about a greater good for you and for others.

Your Story

I firmly believe that my entire story is important, and so is yours. Your story is incredibly significant. And so are you.

That may be a tough statement for you to believe right now. Abuse has a way of blinding us to our own value. You are probably exhausted. You may feel defeated and isolated. When we experience abuse, our tendency is to withdraw into a dark, private corner, fearful that anyone may further hurt or destroy us. And for those who do not withdraw physically, certainly many withdraw emotionally.

At this point, you may feel as if you have little belief left in you. How can you believe in anything when you are broken and empty, with no energy left to imagine life can ever get better? Or maybe you're wondering if you will ever feel joy, peace, or happiness again. How can you believe there is hope? How can you believe in a life after abuse?

I want to take your hand and help you out of that place. I want you to know you are in a safe space, that I care about who you are and where you have been. If I could sit down with you today, over a cup of coffee, I would encourage you with this: it's time to tell your story, at least to yourself. You're ready. And God is on your side. Understandably, some of you may be struggling to believe that God is on your side. Experiencing abuse can leave us feeling distant from Him or questioning if He cares at all. (This is a very important subject that I cover later in the book.)

One of my clients put it this way: "Now that I've begun to talk with you about my story and write about it, I no longer feel like a character in somebody else's story. I used to see my husband as so much larger than life. I thought someday books would be written about him, and I'd be 'his wife.' I'm only beginning to understand that my story is *mine*. I'm learning that many women feel that way—that we are supporting characters in somebody else's story. But that's not the truth."

Your First Step toward Freedom: Telling Your Story

In my own life, God used what felt and looked like a personal failure to bring about something beautiful. I am living proof. Miracles are not just for Jesus's time. They still happen today. My children and I are a living testimony to the fact that not only do miracles happen, but they are also not intended to be kept in a box for ourselves. Instead, we can choose to share our stories with others. By telling our stories, we can discover that our pain has purpose.

That is why I am telling my story. And that is why I encourage you to tell yours when you're ready.

"It was tough at first for me to tell my story," Kate said as she fiddled with a Kleenex on her lap. "I felt like people would judge me and that it would bring shame. But I've experienced just the opposite. Sharing what I went through with people I trust has been not just healing for me but also beneficial for others. I had no idea other people were hiding pain like this too. It's been so freeing!"

The good news is that Jesus wants to set us free (John 8:36; Galatians 5:1). He provides freedom for everyone who chooses it. It is my hope that you will choose it for yourself. What Christ has done for me, He wants to and will do for you. You were created to be loved, respected, valued, and treasured. Life can be tough for all of us at times, but intimate relationships by design are meant to be safe havens, places of refuge. Anything short of that is not God's desire for you. He sees you as the "apple of his eye" (Psalm 17:8). If your experience runs contrary to this, it's time to consider new possibilities, a new way of living and loving. Love is never supposed to involve abuse. This includes you.

Your first step, telling your story, is not easy or simple. I have walked down that road of isolation and fear. You may feel discouraged or even reluctant to believe that this horrible time in your life will ever end and that you can experience peace and happiness again. I understand. I have been there too.

But now I am standing on the other side with the assurance that healing is possible. There is life after abuse. A good life awaits you. One of my favorite verses from the Bible says, "Weeping may last through the night, but joy comes with the morning" (Psalm 30:5 NLT). I am so thankful for this promise, and it can be your promise too. While our stories may be filled with weeping, we can be assured that "joy comes with the morning."

Cling with me to this promise as we walk this journey together. Take my hand. Now let's begin.

Questions to Ponder

At this point in every chapter, I'd like you to write out your thoughts. If you do not have a journal, now is the perfect time to start one. This is your space to be honest, to say what is actually on your heart and mind. Record what has happened, put your stake in the ground, mark where you are, and watch how you will grow.

Please be aware that what you share in this journal needs to be private. You will want to keep it in a safe place. If you know that it will never be read by anyone else, you will find the freedom to speak truth without fear.

Take the time right now to begin writing your story. Even if what you actually put to paper is brief, even if it is just the start of your story, that's okay. It's important that you see something written out. Your story matters. You matter.

Here are some questions to help you get started:

1. Begin writing your story today. You may want to include the following points:

   a. How did the two of you meet?

   b. What attracted you to him?

   c. Can you identify some things in your life that may have caused a void that you thought perhaps he could fill (such as family-of-origin experiences and belief systems)?

    d. Early on, what were some of the things he said and did that were warning signs that you may not be able to trust him with your heart?

       As difficult as it may be, I encourage you to utilize the abuse evaluation form (refer to appendix A). Circle every word or phrase listed on that form that describes what you have experienced in your relationship (even if it happened "only once").

    e. Add anything else you think is important to your story to include at this time.

2. Do you believe it's possible for you to heal well from the pain you have experienced in your relationship?

3. When you reflect on the concept of freedom as it applies to an intimate partner relationship, what would it look like for you? How does your current experience compare?

4. Are you willing to invest the time in yourself to heal well and live free? If this decision is a struggle, I encourage you to believe that you are worth it.

Prayer of Reflection

At the end of each chapter, I'd like to offer a prayer for you to read and meditate on. I hope it will be just a start, the nudge you need to pray on your own. Perhaps you are a person of prayer and turn to God regularly with your deepest hurts and concerns. Or you may be someone who struggles with belief in God, especially in light of the pain you are experiencing. But for now, will you give me permission to pray with you here, to give you a start, to open the door to encourage you to be honest before God? Prayer is simply talking with God. It's a way for you to share your deepest hurts and emotions with Him. You can tell God, honestly, what is on your heart. Pray with me. Unburden yourself before God and know that He hears and that He cares for you.

God, I'm scared. There's a brokenness inside me that feels beyond repair. My life has not turned out as I had hoped. I trusted and loved someone who betrayed me and bruised me in ways that only You can see. It is so painful to think about my own story. It feels almost unbearable. Help me to believe that I can heal—not just heal but heal well. Your Word says that You, Jesus, died so I can be free. Show me how this translates in my life. I am not sure how to be free or where to begin. But You do. You know me. You know my story. You alone can heal my broken heart. Today I place my heart, my hopes, and my life into Your safe hands. The safest place I can be is with You. Your Word promises that You will never leave me. Thank You for loving me even when I doubt You, when I feel abandoned and so alone. You're with me now. Please take my hand and walk me through this journey to healing well. Together, we can do this. Amen.

God's Enduring Promises

You may be very familiar with the Bible, or this might be the first time you've ever read it. No matter what your personal faith journey looks like, I'd like to share some of the Bible passages that were helpful to me. There were times when I read these verses over and over again, through tears, clinging to the hope that they promise.

> I am sick at heart.
> How long, O LORD, until you restore me?
> Return, O LORD, and rescue me.
> Save me because of your unfailing love.

For the dead do not remember you.
  Who can praise you from the grave?
I am worn out from sobbing.
  All night I flood my bed with weeping,
    drenching it with my tears.
My vision is blurred by grief;
  my eyes are worn out because of all my enemies.
Go away, all you who do evil,
  for the Lord has heard my weeping.
The Lord has heard my plea;
  the Lord will answer my prayer. (Psalm 6:3–9 NLT)

But you, God, see the trouble of the afflicted;
  you consider their grief and take it in hand.
The victims commit themselves to you;
  you are the helper of the fatherless. (Psalm 10:14)

I call on you, my God, for you will answer me;
  turn your ear to me and hear my prayer.
Show me the wonders of your great love,
  you who save by your right hand
    those who take refuge in you from their foes.
Keep me as the apple of your eye;
  hide me in the shadow of your wings
from the wicked who are out to destroy me,
  from my mortal enemies who surround me. (Psalm
    17:6–9)

He reached down from heaven and rescued me;
  he drew me out of deep waters.
He rescued me from my powerful enemies,
  from those who hated me and were too strong for me.
They attacked me at a moment when I was in distress,
  but the Lord supported me.
He led me to a place of safety;
  he rescued me because he delights in me. (Psalm 18:16–
    19 NLT)

So if the Son sets you free, you will be free indeed. (John 8:36)

It is for freedom that Christ has set us free. Stand firm, then, and do not let yourselves be burdened again by a yoke of slavery. (Galatians 5:1)

2

Breaking the Silence

People asked me all the time if I was all right," Amber said. "Not close friends—I didn't have any of those—just people we'd see at my children's school or the doctor's office or whatever. Truth was I was always sick with some illness or another. The stress of living with an abuser had wrecked my immune system. I got this question often, but I didn't feel I could tell the whole truth of how I really was—that the violence at home was literally making me sick."

Amber confessed this during one of our sessions. And I knew immediately what she was talking about.

I remember staring at my own reflection in the mirror years ago and recognizing my face but not the person I had become. *How did I get here?* I wondered. My zest for life and my dreams for the future were distant memories. I'd spent so many years in the throes of a tumultuous relationship, and the only good things I had to show for it were my beautiful children and the fact that I was still alive. I'd become totally disconnected from my family, my friends, and pretty much life in general.

The Secret

The violence in our home was the Big Secret. Ben had warned me repeatedly that if I told anyone, especially the police, "someone would be dead."

Keeping the secret is the lifeblood of the horrendous abuse cycle. Make no mistake: secrets are toxic! In the shadow of the secret, the abuse will continue and most often will get worse. Abusers need secrecy to cloak their actions and their dual lives. They are Mr. Wonderful in the public eye but Mr. Monster at home. Secrecy keeps outsiders from knowing the hell that lurks behind the front door.

If it's so bad, and it is, why do we continue to keep the secret?

In my own life, I was enamored with Ben's "good side." I was blindsided by who he really was. This was not the man I had married. He had a very tender side. But his other side was gruff, entitled, dangerous, and desensitized. This dual nature threw me into a tailspin that lasted for years. I hung in there, thinking, *Surely his good side will remain this time*. This time never came.

Looking back, I realize I too was living a dual life. I appeared all put together, and I felt enormous pressure to keep everything going for the sake of our family. On the outside, I came across as confident and strong, when, in fact, my private world was an entirely different story. The secret allowed me to keep this façade going. And I believed that if I could keep it going long enough, it would eventually become reality.

But the biggest reason I kept the secret for so many years? I loved him. I didn't want people to think badly of him. I erroneously believed that I could work on the marriage privately and not damage our reputation. The fact is the abuse continued to happen over and over again.

The Mind Bender

Breaking the silence is key to interrupting the cycle. It opens a world of new possibilities, health, freedom, safety, and new life.

This step can be pretty scary, I know. But it's so important.

In the last chapter, we talked about the need to tell your story. I encouraged you to think about how you got to this place and to begin writing it down. The next step is to find a safe person with whom to share your story.

Be advised that breaking the silence is not necessarily synonymous with leaving the abuser. Some of my clients worry about breaking the silence, fearing they're not capable of doing both at the same time. The emotional cost is just too high, and they need time. Let me reiterate that breaking the silence is about telling your story first to yourself, then to a safe person. Breaking the silence is not necessarily about leaving your abusive partner right now, although for some, it may be. If you are considering leaving now, please refer to appendix B for safety plans and to appendix C for professional support to assist you.

The decision to entrust your story to someone can feel overwhelming. Fear has been used to manipulate and silence you, so it can seem almost inconceivable that you could actually share your story with someone. You may wonder, *Will anyone believe me?* This question can be exceptionally scary the longer the secret has been kept and the degree to which the secret has isolated you from family and friends.

"Andy was respected and loved in our community," Kate confided recently. "He seemed to be so kind to all his employees, to people in the neighborhood, really to everyone he met. Wait staff would rush over to serve us in restaurants. Our lifestyle was pretty expensive, and people thought I was the luckiest woman in town, but he controlled every single penny and every moment of my time. If I even hinted at trouble at home, I paid for it dearly behind closed doors. I learned to smile and laugh even when I was bruised and reeling from his treatment the night before. Who would believe me when everyone liked him so much?"

Kate's description of this mind bender between what appears to be and what is rings true for most people who are in an abusive relationship. You can feel delusional as your abuser insists that what is going on isn't really happening. You're the crazy one rather than the abused one.

Abusers almost always present themselves one way to outsiders and another way in the privacy of their own homes. Many are super likeable, charismatic, and charming. Socially, they have great acumen and often come across as rescuers, which is commendable. They have a larger-than-life, hero-like reputation. As a result, you may be concerned that some family members and friends won't fully believe your story or may not believe it at all.

Perhaps, like me, you come from a family that does not condone divorce. I was taught growing up that husbands and wives stay together no matter what. Divorce was not an option in my parents' minds, so I somehow accepted I had to suffer until Ben changed. And as I described above, Ben saved his "other side" for me and our kids. My family never had the pleasure of experiencing Mr. Monster.

But there comes a moment when each of us realizes that the cost of maintaining the secret is too high a price to pay. What leads to that moment can be very different for each person. What's crucial is not so much why you break the silence but that you do.

The Day I Broke the Silence

For me, that moment came when I sat across the table from a dear woman I'd just met. She was a financial coach who assisted people with putting their finances back on track. In my marriage, money was always a huge source of contention. I wanted to save, and Ben wanted to spend, spend, spend. As a result of our joint credit cards, my credit was a disaster. As I tentatively shared bits of my story with her, she politely interrupted me and asked, "When are you going to say, 'Enough!'?" I looked back at her as if to say, "I didn't know I could ever say, 'Enough!' I can?"

I'd left with my children sometimes for several hours, sometimes for a few days, sometimes for a couple weeks. But Ben was always able to persuade me to come back. (I will address why victims of domestic violence stay or return to their abusers in a later chapter.) Until that moment, the idea of saying, "No more, I will not tolerate this kind of treatment," did not seem like an option to me. But in reality, it was.

So sitting there that day with a woman I barely knew, I made a decision. I wanted a different life for me and my children. I was done believing empty promises of change and having hope in illusive happiness. I finally admitted to myself that Ben did not want to change and never intended to change. And I had to accept his decision. But more importantly, I needed to make a decision for myself. On that afternoon, sitting in a booth at Chili's, I decided I was the one who was going to change.

Instinctively, I just sort of knew I could trust this woman with a few morsels of my story. I broke the silence. I told someone outside my circle of secrecy. I will forever be grateful to her for her gift of believing me. She empowered me by challenging me to believe that my life could change. I could actually say, "No more."

Find Your Safe Person

"I told my sister first, but she didn't believe me," Kate confessed. "So I sort of figured nobody would believe me if my own sister didn't. But one day someone at the doctor's office asked me about a gash I had on my arm, and, I don't know, something about her told me I could trust her. She listened without judging and gave me the number of a domestic violence counselor. She said, 'You don't deserve to be mistreated like that. You deserve better.' I immediately called the women's shelter when I left the doctor's office, before I could lose my nerve. And that made all the difference."

Like Kate, once you tell your story to your safe person, I encourage you to seek help from a professional counselor who understands the complexities of domestic violence, also known as intimate partner violence. You do not need to do so the same day, but you will benefit from the wise counsel and support of a trained professional. If you are not in a position to afford private counseling, call one of the hotlines listed in appendix C. Whoever answers can advise you on resources in your area. Many shelters offer support groups that can provide you with information and a safe place to begin the healing process.

Resist the temptation at this point to minimize your experience by calling the abuse "just normal couple conflict." Every couple has challenges, but not every couple experiences abuse. What I am addressing in this book is not typical marital or couple difficulties (i.e., more month than money, teething babies, opinionated teenagers, or difficult in-laws, to mention a few). We are speaking here of something else: abuse. (Please refer to appendix D for a list of various types of abuse.) There is *never* a justification for abuse of any kind in any relationship. When you realize what you are dealing with and you reach the place where you decide this is not the life you want for yourself or your children, this is the moment when a professional, trained ear is crucial. You need someone who understands abuse in the context of an intimate relationship.

And most importantly, you need someone who will believe you. Your story is real. Your experiences are true. You deserve to be believed. In choosing a counselor, make sure they have been adequately trained. If they even hint at couple's counseling, run for the hills! They don't know what they are doing. This is not a couple's issue. This is not a communication problem or a need to learn conflict resolution. When one person exerts power and control over another, it is abuse.

A few questions to ask a potential counselor are:

- Do you have specific training in treating victims of domestic violence?
- Are you trained to work with those suffering from PTSD as a result of the trauma an abusive relationship can cause?
- In the case of suspected domestic violence, do you recommend couple's counseling? (If they say yes, keep looking!)

So often I meet with women who are determined to help their significant other change and to save the marriage, but in the end, the question is not "Is the marriage worth saving?" but "Am I worth saving?"

Believe me, you are worth saving!

It all starts with this first commitment you make to yourself: **I deserve to be valued and treated with kindness and respect.** Decide to accept that abuse of any kind is intolerable. Decide to embrace what you know to be true as opposed to what appears to be true even if it means no longer hoping that things will work out. Surrender your dreams of what your family and your future could look like. Let go of the façade . . . and it begins with breaking the silence.

How do you break the silence?

You tell your story.

Questions to Ponder

1. How has the secret hurt you? How has it hurt your children? How has living in an abusive relationship affected your other relationships?

2. Are you ready to say, "Enough!"? If yes, why? If no, why not?

3. Are you willing to find a trusted and trained counselor to join you in the steps to healing well?

Prayer of Reflection

God, I see more clearly now how secrecy has become my norm. Out of fear of what might happen, what others might think, and even my own denial regarding the severity of my situation, I have kept the secret. On the outside, we look fine, but behind closed doors, it is an entirely different reality. I find comfort in knowing that I can tell You the truth and that You listen to me without judgment. Please help me, Lord, to come to a place where I can share my story with a safe person. Please bring someone into my life who will believe me and who will not judge me. Protect me and my children when I finally do break the silence. Give me courage and give me strength to no longer minimize the abuse. Amen.

God's Enduring Promises

Then Jesus said, "Come to me, all of you who are weary and carry heavy burdens, and I will give you rest." (Matthew 11:28 NLT)

> For he has not despised or scorned
> the suffering of the afflicted one;
> he has not hidden his face from him
> but has listened to his cry for help. (Psalm 22:24)

> In you, Lord my God,
> I put my trust.
> I trust in you;
> do not let me be put to shame,
> nor let my enemies triumph over me.
> No one who hopes in you
> will ever be put to shame,
> but shame will come on those
> who are treacherous without cause.

Show me your ways, Lord,
  teach me your paths.
Guide me in your truth and teach me,
  for you are God my Savior,
  and my hope is in you all day long. (Psalm 25:1–5)

3

Call It What It Is . . . Abuse

When my son was young, he'd be out playing and would return home with one of "God's little creatures," as we called them. He'd cup his newfound friend in mud-covered hands and name it Jack. Basically, anything that crossed his little Tom Sawyer path became Jack. We had Jack the turtle, Jack the wooly bear caterpillar, Jack the garter snake, and Jack the tree frog. Once he referred to his new companion with this name, it was coming home to stay.

There is tremendous significance in giving something a name. Naming can denote value, meaning, a sense of responsibility, even ownership. And until we call things what they are, we deny their true impact, and their meaning in our lives remains unclear.

Before I realized what I was dealing with in my marriage, I rationalized Ben's behavior by using such excuses as "He has a bad temper," "He's going through a tough time," or one that really makes my stomach turn today, "He isn't a good communicator and doesn't know how to express his emotions." I can remember feeling very sad for him, believing that he was misunderstood by people. I thought it was my responsibility as his wife to dismiss his behavior by inserting one of these excuses. In addition to this, I had the erroneous belief that if I only tried harder, loved him more, looked prettier, prayed more, had more faith . . . then he would love me and treat me with tenderness. And most importantly, I held out the hope that my love and loyalty would convince him to change.

One night I got up while Ben was still sleeping to do a Google search of a term my best friend had encouraged me to read about. The term was *cycle of abuse*. I remember like it was yesterday how my hand on the computer mouse shook as I read the information. In those early morning hours, I read the definition and realized I was smack in the middle of a very toxic pattern. For the first time in my marriage, I knew what I was experiencing had a name . . . *Abuse*.

One of my clients tells the story of how she attempted to name the abuse in her own marriage. After talking to a counselor who used the word to describe what seemed to be happening in her marriage, Jane brought it up with her husband. "He flew off the handle, asked how I could hurt him like that, and threatened to harm himself. I never brought it up again . . . until the day I left with a black eye four years later." Naming what was happening in their home put the onus back where it belonged—on the abuser. He couldn't stand that, so he shifted the blame.

Like me and Jane, some women enduring intimate partner violence falsely believe theirs is a marital problem, in other words, a couple's issue. Holding on to this belief gives victims a false sense of control. After all, if I was part of the reason Ben behaved the way he did, then I could somehow stop it. Let's be clear: the only person with control over the abuse is the abuser. Contrary to what we may have been told or have told ourselves in the past, we cannot break the abuse cycle with better behavior, more prayer, less cellulite, or a tastier meat loaf.

Abuse is not something you can manage or control. Accepting this is paramount to having a clear understanding that it is solely your abuser's choice to abuse and that you are not responsible for his behavior. This understanding also completely eradicates the very common and dangerous misconception that somehow you provoked him and he had no other choice than to "set you straight." As long as you believe you are somehow responsible for your abuser's behavior, you will remain in the tangled web of abuse.

So what drives an abuser's behavior?

The Mind-set of an Abuser: Entitlement

An abuser's mind-set, not his anger, drives his behavior. An abuser does not have an anger problem. He has an entitlement problem. He believes he is entitled to control and will do what he can to achieve and maintain it, regardless of the cost. The same man who hits his wife or calls her horrible names is capable of showing up at work the next day and minding his p's and q's with his female boss or associate. Now this does not mean he has true respect for his female boss. But what it clearly shows is that he saves his abusive behavior exclusively for his intimate partner. Hence the name: intimate partner violence.

It was during my doctoral program, as I was writing my dissertation on the topic of domestic violence in faith-based relationships, that I discovered an author who did a fabulous job of debunking many of the myths surrounding this issue as well as explaining how entitlement and lack of empathy fuel an abusive mentality. His name is Lundy Bancroft. He started the nation's first program working with male abusers almost thirty years ago. He wrote *Why Does He Do That? Inside the Minds of Angry and Controlling Men*. I encourage you to read it. As part of my research studies, I flew to Boston to interview this author. It was a gorgeous fall day in New England, and due to a last-minute change of plans, we conducted the interview on his mother's back porch. At the end of the interview, I told Lundy I had one final question to ask him.

I said, "Why is it that some men abuse?" I thought he was going to give me some long, prolific answer. He didn't. He simply said, "Because they can."

You see, abuse has a payoff—it is effective as far as the abuser is concerned. The payoff is often not apparent to the untrained eye, but there are definitely rewards built into this often very confusing and complicated dynamic. For example, power and control, getting his way, and having you to take his problems out on are just a few of the rewards the abuser gains. (See appendix H for a more comprehensive list.) The abuser abuses, the victim responds, the cycle continues . . . sometimes for a lifetime. And until the victim realizes that what she does not know is hurting her immensely and has the potential to end her very life, round and round the two people will continue.

"My husband would call me at work with some dramatic tale of what was happening to him—a broken-down car, a relationship crisis at his work, something that he said needed my attention," Kate shared with me recently. "Early on in our relationship, I thought this was his way of leaning on me, of my being a good partner to him. But he had this way of always making his crisis somehow more critical than whatever I was doing. And if I challenged him or somehow showed reluctance to prioritize his problem over mine, he'd be enraged and question my love and loyalty to him."

Because of the entitlement mind-set of an abuser, he will always prioritize his needs over yours.

The Mind-set of an Abuser: Lack of Empathy

An abuser lacks true empathy on a normative scale. He refuses to see his behavior from his partner's perspective, although he will most likely deny this. And he also refuses to acknowledge how his behavior impacts his partner.

I recall vividly early on in our marriage when I was sick with the flu. After an entire night of vomiting and sleeping on the floor next to the toilet, I made a simple request: "Ben, can you please bring me a glass of orange juice?" To which he quickly retorted, "Get up and get it yourself!" Years later when I asked Ben about his response, he told me I was crazy and that he never said such a thing. He showed a lack of empathy and denial in full force.

Abusers externalize their responsibility by making you the reason or cause for their abusive behavior. The rational, although faulty, is the same. If you are to blame, then you are the reason he behaves the way he does. If you are the reason, then you have the power to stop the cycle. As we discussed, abusive behavior is fueled by a mind-set that includes both entitlement and lack of empathy. He believes that he is entitled to say and do the things he says and does. When that results in a verbal, emotional, sexual, or physical assault, then it's your fault. After one particular incident when Ben gave me a black eye, he actually insisted, "You gave it to yourself!" Have you ever heard anything as preposterous as that? Who gives herself a black eye? How do you even give yourself a black eye?

An abuser lacks sincere empathy for the pain he caused. In his twisted mind-set, if you deserved it, why should he feel sorry for his actions? He doesn't. When the honeymoon phase circles back, as the cycle of abuse spins round, he may bring flowers or gifts or perform acts of contrition. He may seem sincere at the moment. You will want to believe his apparent remorse is true. However, it begs the question, "If he is truly sorry and promises never to do it again, why does he?" The answer never changes, "It's because he can."

This is precisely where I encourage you to ask yourself, "Is this what I want for myself?" My prayer is that at this point your conviction is, "Enough is enough!"

You Can't Change His Behavior, but You Can Change Yours

A healthy response at this point is to let go of the false belief that somehow, someway, with some miracle, you can change him. The truth is that if he is going to change, he is going to have to do it himself. We do not have the power to change another person regardless of how hard we try. Frankly, it is hard enough to change ourselves.

What I have come to understand is that it was only through God's grace in my life that I was finally able to change, meaning I changed my focus from trying to help Ben change to prioritizing myself and my children. In the end, it was me who changed. I had to acknowledge the faulty thinking that skewed my perception.

The sad truth is that an abuser seldom changes. His behavior rewards him with what he thinks he wants: control. This "reward" comes with a very high price though. He inevitably drives away, if not physically then certainly emotionally, the very person he intended to be closest with. If the victim does not eventually leave, which many victims do, she will definitely detach from him emotionally because it is not safe for her to trust him. Without trust, there is no relationship. Trust must be fostered in an environment that is safe. So when this house of cards finally comes crashing down, she is left with the wreckage, the broken pieces of what she hoped would be a happily ever after ending. The result is that this fairy tale turned horror film leaves the victim with nothing in the end but raw grief.

When We Grieve Well, We Heal Well

When you have told your story, broken the silence, and called it what it is (abuse), you will realize that this person is not likely to change. In my experience, this realization will lead to grief. Grief, by definition, is a signal that something is over. It is the very essence of loss. It is a natural and normal response. Any attempt to avoid grief will impede the healing process, causing you to feel stuck rather than pass through this necessary response to loss. When I finally accepted my marriage to Ben was over, I cried constantly and in situations where doing so wasn't appropriate, such as in the classroom in front of my peers. I would politely excuse myself, go sit in my car, and wait for the wave of emotion to pass.

Grieving is very painful. It can be an incredibly lonely journey. In my private practice, I always encourage my grieving clients to resist the temptation to run from or numb their grief. They need to allow themselves to feel their deep emotions in order to heal well. So do you. A myriad of emotions will flood you, sometimes multiple times in one day. Grief is often comprised of the following phases, though not necessarily in this order: shock, denial, anger, bargaining, depression, acceptance.

My client Amber said it this way: "I was reading a self-help book on marriage when it became clear that I was stuck in the cycle of abuse. I immediately went into denial. I even went so far as to day-dream about a recommitment ceremony with my husband. But then I literally tore up the paper I was doodling details on. I was on a trip for work and literally could not get out of bed for the meetings. When I finally rallied that afternoon, I was so filled with anger at my situation that I went for a long run—and I wasn't even an athlete at the time!"

The shock you feel when you realize the situation you are in often gives way to denial. You want to pretend that what you know to be true is not. Denial is best buddies with bargaining, in which you "if only" yourself to death. When bargaining doesn't provide any real answers, you can find yourself steeped in depression. And the emotion that tends to blanket them all is anger. This anger can often feel like rage because the person who promised to love you "till death do us part" was the very person who broke your heart. This pain can leave you feeling so raw that the thought that your life can ever feel like living again seems like a sinister fantasy at best.

Grief is rarely experienced in a nice, neat, linear way. Grieving is messy work. One moment you may feel angry and the next depressed. After depression lifts, you may find yourself right back at bargaining. The good news—and there is good news—is that as you permit yourself to feel, then you allow yourself to heal.

You cannot heal from what you will not feel, and you cannot feel what you will not talk about. Sharing your story gives wings to your words and in time lifts the painful emotions from your heart, freeing you to embrace life again.

Grieving is the doorway through which you eventually find freedom . . . if you do not give up on the process. Healing well makes you stronger by helping you to accept the various parts of your life experiences, not in the sense that you accept the abuse in some twisted sort of way but that you recognize the power of integrating the good, the bad, and the very ugly into your story, which ultimately will bring you from victim to survivor!

Questions to Ponder

1. Other than calling it what it is, what names, phrases, or terminology have you used to describe the abuse you have experienced?

2. What feelings are generated when you call it what it is: abuse?

3. Now that you understand that in order for you to heal you need to feel, and you connect with your feelings by sharing your story, where do you see yourself in this process?

4. Permitting yourself to grieve is crucial to healing well. Are you allowing yourself to grieve, or are you substituting true grieving with other distractions?

5. Do you see indications of shock, denial, anger, bargaining, and/or depression in your journey as you continue to heal well?

Prayer of Reflection

Reading this book is not easy for me. Many times I have wanted to put it down and not pick it up again. But You,

Jesus, continue to call my name. I hear You whispering for me to come sit with You and to allow You to comfort me. Calling it what it is has been one of the toughest steps for me. Because once I call it what it is, then I am faced with a decision. I have to decide whether I am worth what it will take to heal well and eventually live free again. Abuse is a serious word. It's much more serious than having "an issue" or "a challenge." Everyone has those. But abuse is different. No one deserves to be abused. That includes me.

How I got here and how I allowed this in my life are hard for me to understand. But I know that if I continue to minimize what I see and what I know to be true, I will never heal, and my life will never change. I want to heal. I want to change. Please help me, Jesus, to continue calling it what it is. I see the cycle. Tension builds, explosion happens, empty promises are made. Nothing changes. This is not what I want for my life. This is not how I want to live. Please enable me, Jesus, to no longer deny what I see. Give me strength and give me courage to call it what it is from this day forward. Amen.

God's Enduring Promises

"If you'll hold on to me for dear life," says GOD,
    "I'll get you out of any trouble.
I'll give you the best of care
    if you'll only get to know and trust me.
Call me and I'll answer, be at your side in bad times;
    I'll rescue you, then throw you a party.
I'll give you a long life,
    give you a long drink of salvation!" (Psalm 91:14–16
    Message)

For God has not given us a spirit of fear, but of power and of love and of a sound mind. (2 Timothy 1:7 NKJV)

> "For I will restore health to you
> And heal you of your wounds," says the LORD,
> "Because they called you an outcast saying:
> 'This is Zion;
> No one seeks her.'" (Jeremiah 30:17 NKJV)

> Heal me, O LORD, and I will be healed;
> Save me and I will be saved,
> For You are my praise. (Jeremiah 17:14 AMP)

4

Why the Pain Outlasts
the Bruises

When you read about the terrible night Ben attacked me, driving his thumbs into my eye sockets, I suspect you were hoping for me to be rescued somehow, hoping for a change. The fact is our human nature recognizes this kind of mistreatment and knows it's not right. And yet abused women stay with men who abuse them, year after year, suffering in the nightmare, yearning for change, just as I did.

Believe me, as a therapist, I've seen both women and men stay in abusive situations even when they've suffered in unconscionable ways. Having experienced physical harm, verbal assaults, emotional sabotage, sexual deviance, or even spiritual manipulation, they often do not recognize it for what it is. Abuse, simply put, is malevolent control. No human being should have to stay in a relationship in which abuse is present. And yet, people do. Because when you love someone, you hope for healing, change, and reconciliation.

When someone you love is an abuser, they don't initially present as such. But over time, you realized what he is, although you may not have wanted to believe it because there were good times as well. Throughout the years I've been in practice, I have heard clients minimize the abuse. "He only hit me once, and that was years ago. He's sworn he won't do it again, but his anger keeps me on edge," Kate recently confided. "He's not really abusing me every day. But I'm afraid."

The fact is abuse exists on a very long continuum. It can be anything from a threatening stare that clearly says, "Shut up or else!" to a ferocious physical attack that results in death. Initially, abuse is often exhibited in more subtle ways such as sarcasm, name-calling, or put-downs. However, it *always* gets worse with time.

My early dating years with Ben were pure bliss, but this did not last. Ben eventually started to call me names like "idiot" and "stupid," and he occasionally would throw a "you're crazy" comment in there. Still starry-eyed and completely smitten, I naïvely ignored these warning signs that danger was looming. What did I do instead? I drew up a contract. You heard me right. I wrote a contract indicating the words that we (notice I incriminated myself, even though I never referred to him with such terms) would refrain from using with each other. I included words such as *idiot, stupid, dumb, crazy*, and anything else I thought I needed to cover. I dated the contract, and we both signed it. What a waste that was. Not only was my hope that he would uphold his "promise" never to call me names a complete flop, but he also escalated from names like "idiot" and "stupid" to those like "whore" and "bitch." Believe me when I tell you, abuse always gets worse over time.

The Cycle of Abuse: A Predictable Pattern

Lenore Walker, an American psychologist who founded the Domestic Violence Institute, wrote *The Battered Woman*. For the book, she interviewed fifteen hundred victims of domestic violence and found that there was a pattern of behavior in abusive relationships. She referred to this pattern as the Cycle Theory of

Violence, which is commonly referred to as the Cycle of Violence or Cycle of Abuse. For this book, I have adapted Lenore's ideas into my own diagram showing the Cycle of Abuse. Inside of each phase—tension-building, explosion, and honeymoon—common behaviors of both victims (V) and abusers (A) are listed (see appendix E for additional information).

Explosion Phase

Triggering Incident

A: Emotionally, physically, psychologically, sexually, and/or verbally abuses

V: Leaves, fights back, tries to reason with abuser, calls police, tries to protect herself and kids

A: Is moody, yells, threatens, criticizes, plays mind games, withdraws affection

V: Nurtures, is agreeable, feels tension, attempts to calm abuser, stays away from others

Denial

V: Stops legal proceedings, returns to relationship, sets up counseling, feels hopeful

A: Makes promises, gives gifts, says "I'm sorry," promises to attend counseling

Tension-Building Phase

Honeymoon Phase

V = Victim's Behaviors
A = Abuser's Behaviors

For some, the cycle can happen hundreds of times, while for others, it may take months or a year or more to come full circle. Many notice that the length of the cycle diminishes over time because the honeymoon or reconciliation period ceases to exist. Yet the violence becomes more intense and the cycles more frequent.

The cycle begins with the tension-building phase. This is the time during which the victim often feels as if she is walking on eggshells. "My husband just got a new job," a client said recently. "It's been really tough on him. I'm just trying not to rock the boat because I know he could go off at any moment. He has such a short fuse." As the tension mounts between them, the victim attempts to keep the abuser calm, well aware that an explosion is imminent. A triggering incident leads to the explosion phase, when some form of abuse is inflicted upon the victim.

After the explosion phase, the honeymoon phase inevitably follows. During this time, the abuser makes promises he will not keep, minimizes his abusive behavior, or even acts as if the abuse never happened. Often he blames the victim, stating that she did something that caused him to behave this way. Or he gives gifts in an attempt to make up. Then the tension-building stage begins again.

Since Walker's discoveries in 1979, others have built on her initial observations regarding common patterns in abusive relationships. Although many who experience abuse in their intimate relationships can identify with the phases Walker described, not everyone witnesses the same pattern. Regardless of how the cycle plays out, what matters most is that you realize abuse never plateaus.

The Pain That Outlasts the Bruises: PTSD

The trauma of experiencing the cycle of abuse often leads to a condition known as post-traumatic stress disorder, or PTSD. When I see a client exhibiting symptoms of PTSD, I'm reminded of how the emotional wounds resulting from trauma often outlast the injuries. The pain that we tuck deep down inside ourselves can endure long after the injuries have healed. Whether it produces bruises to the body or bruises to the heart, abuse of any kind always leaves an aftermath that cannot be ignored. Our pain demands to be heard. Most importantly, our pain can teach us if we will entrust ourselves to the healing process. It is not uncommon for victims of domestic violence to exhibit symptoms of PTSD. They include the following:

- *Behavioral symptoms*: agitation, irritability, hostility, hyper-vigilance, self-destructive behavior, avoidance of situations that remind the victim of the event(s), difficulty expressing feelings, trouble concentrating, or social isolation
- *Psychological symptoms*: flashbacks (reliving the traumatic event or events), fear, severe anxiety, feelings of being constantly on edge, unwanted thoughts, or mistrust
- *Physical symptoms for no reason you can think of (called somatic complaints)*: nausea, tremors, pain, fainting, dizziness, headache, stomachache, vomiting, or other physical symptoms
- *Mood-related symptoms*: loss of interest or pleasure in activities, guilt, emotional numbness, emotional detachment, or loneliness
- *Sleep-related symptoms*: insomnia, nightmares, or night terrors (resembles a panic attack, but the victim is asleep)

The majority of people who experience relationship abuse exhibit some degree of PTSD. Research has shown that the trauma that results from exposure to domestic violence mimics the trauma that war veterans exhibit from exposure to war. The main difference is that a victim of domestic violence faces the enemy in her own home as opposed to on a battlefield. Living day in and day out never knowing when another emotional, verbal, or physical grenade will be thrown at you takes its toll. That toll is PTSD. And that is why working with a trained domestic violence counselor can be life altering in your pursuit of healing well.

In my own experience, the impact of counseling was astounding. I have found that it is crucial to work with someone who understands the complexities surrounding this issue. In addition to understanding the trauma that results from domestic violence, the professional you choose needs to be a good fit. Simply put, you should feel comfortable with them, feel understood by them, and feel validated regarding the impact abuse has had on you.

Abuse Has Changed You

Several years into my marriage, my youngest brother flew out to visit us. The night before he was to fly back home, we took a long walk along the Chattahoochee River. I'll never forget what happened. About halfway through our walk, he gently took me by the shoulders and asked, "What's wrong with you?" I quickly replied, "Nothing is wrong with me." If you knew this brother of mine, you would know he's not someone you can brush off. He continued by saying, "Something's not right with you. You've lost your moxie." My moxie, as he put it, had long since vanished. The years of abuse were taking their toll much more than I realized. My brother remembered me as someone with a zest for life, full of energy and spunk. He saw the change that was taking place in me even though I was not yet ready to see it. Because my extended family lived on the West Coast and my husband and I had moved to the South, it would often be months, and sometimes even an entire year, before we saw each other. And besides, there was no way I was about to tell them what was happening in our home. I kept the secret like it was a well-guarded tomb, not realizing at the time that it was me I was burying.

The effects of abuse are enormous, but like the proverbial frog in the pot, you may not realize that your life is at a boiling point until after you're scorched. That is what happened to me. You may not be aware of how much you have changed. How your outlook on life, the goals and dreams you once held so dear, and even perhaps the core of who you really are have been altered as a result of trauma. Recognizing your own trauma is crucial. Ignoring the effects the abuse has had on you will affect every area of your life. You will never be able to push the memories so far out of your mind that they no longer affect you. It's impossible. Trust me, if it were possible, I surely would have found a way. I became a master at hiding the truth from myself and from others. But the real truth is . . . *you* matter. Your life matters. And I know for certain without ever meeting you that if you have children, they matter greatly to you as well. Know you're on the right track. You chose to pick up this book, and your heart is open to hearing what I have to say. My prayer is that as you continue along your healing path, you will discover what I already know: *you're worth it!*

Questions to Ponder

1. After looking over the examples provided below, list the evidence you observe of the cycle of abuse in your relationship. (Keep in mind that this pattern can quickly cycle through the tension-building, explosion, and honeymoon phases. Or it can take months or even more than a year to fully cycle. The important thing is not how long the pattern takes to come full circle but the fact that it's happening. Please refer to appendix E for a more detailed overview of this cycle.)

Tension-Building Phase	Triggering Incident	Explosion Phase	Honeymoon Phase
Example: I've had a knot in my stomach for weeks. I'm making every effort to keep the kids quiet and not upset him. I avoided talking about bills because I know he will throw a fit.	Example: I had to buy school clothes for the kids and spent more than usual.	Example: He found the receipts in the desk drawer. In a rage, he swiped everything off the top of the desk, including my laptop. He then proceeded to call me a stupid idiot and accuse me of being irresponsible with money. He canceled our dinner plans with friends as well.	Example: I cleaned up the mess in our office. He approached me the next day with a cup of coffee and asked if I wanted to spend the day with my best friend, Lori. He was pleasant and even cut the lawn without me having to ask him.

Tension-Building Phase	Triggering Incident	Explosion Phase	Honeymoon Phase

2. Reread the symptoms of PTSD. What symptoms are you experiencing that may be a direct result of the trauma you have experienced or are continuing to experience?

3. To what extent have your outlook on life, the goals and dreams you once held so dear, and even perhaps the core of who you really are been altered as a result of this trauma?

Prayer of Reflection

For so long, Jesus, I have walked around with this pain inside. I've been hiding my pain from the world and trying even more desperately to hide it from myself. I can no longer carry this pain. The abuse has clearly left its marks on my life. I have changed in many ways, and these changes frighten me. I need Your help. Acknowledging this is difficult for me. Sometimes it feels easier to pretend the changes aren't there. But I feel them. Long after the bruises have faded, the residual effects linger on. The horrible names I've been called, the threats, the assaults have mounted to proportions that I can no longer bear. I know You see it all. You see the bruises that no one sees. You see my tears, both those I have cried and those that are still buried inside. Hold me, Jesus. Hold my heart. It feels broken beyond repair. But You tell me that You are the mender of the brokenhearted. So I come to You. I place my bruised heart and tired body into Your hands. I know that in Your hands is the safest place for me to be. Help me to stay there while You heal the broken places within me that only You can see. Amen.

God's Enduring Promises

> You keep track of all my sorrows.
>> You have collected all my tears in your bottle.
>> You have recorded each one in your book. (Psalm 56:8 NLT)

The Lord is near to those who have a broken heart. And He saves those who are broken in spirit. (Psalm 34:18 NLV)

> Unless the LORD had given me help,
>> I would soon have dwelt in the silence of death.
> When I said, "My foot is slipping,"
>> your unfailing love, LORD, supported me.
> When anxiety was great within me,
>> your consolation brought me joy. (Psalm 94:17–19)

5

Can a Band-Aid Heal a Broken Heart?

When I was a child, I loved to spend summer days riding my bike. The thrill of barreling down the driveway and launching off the dirt ramp my brothers and I had built at the bottom was exhilarating! How we survived childhood amazes me still, and this was before bike helmets! But what happened when I fell off my bike and skinned my knee? I was supposed to stop playing and go inside so my mom could wash it off and put Mercurochrome on it. Remember that horrible stuff? It was a liquid red betadine, kind of like iodine, with an antiseptic in it that stung worse than the original injury! Many times I kept the scraped knee to myself rather than face my mom and her Mercurochrome. Well, years later, if I look closely, I can see scar tissue that grew around those ignored childhood cuts.

Emotional Band-Aids

Childhood scrapes and scratches may have healed without the soapy water and stinging antiseptics, but our scars prove that shortcuts can cost us. Choosing to jump right back up on the bicycle, ignoring the injury, came with a price. Healing is not the same as healing well. Healing well involves allowing the wound to be properly cleaned, perhaps removing little pieces of dirt, and applying uncomfortable medicine in order to avoid infection and future scarring. The same is true emotionally. When we treat our emotional wounds, we may experience some pain as we walk through the process of healing well. But unless we're willing to face, feel, and properly fix our emotional injuries, we will never heal well and certainly will never live free. Hence, what's true in the physical is also true in the emotional. Ignoring emotional pain leaves emotional scars.

A Band-Aid cannot heal a broken heart any more than a Band-Aid can heal a broken arm. Yet so many of us try this approach, which short-circuits our true healing. I was an all-star when it came to doing anything but looking at my pain. I hid behind overachiever, high performer, and Miss Polly Perfect for years. I tried to perform more in order to get Ben to love me more with the assumption I'd feel better. Not! Perfectionism never solves or fixes anything. It won't ever stop the abuse you're experiencing. You can try and try to improve yourself, but improving you will never change him.

My underlying hope was that no one would notice how broken I was inside. I was so worn-out and depleted that to get through the day I drank multiple energy drinks and took B12 injections. Drinking energy drinks may sound like no big deal, but it was much more than that. I would actually hide these drinks from my kids in an effort to protect "my stash." When I say I literally could not make it through the day without massive doses of B vitamins, I'm not kidding. Who hides energy drinks between their couch cushions? Someone who knows that without them they'll collapse. Eventually, I did. My body gave out, and I developed rheumatoid arthritis. My immune system finally went tilt!

Cleaning the house was another Band-Aid for my emotional pain. Many times after Ben would destroy furniture or break something I valued, I would vacuum straight lines into the carpet, hoping to suck up the desperation I felt and control the chaos. I can still remember the aah feeling I felt as I vacuumed line after straight line into the carpet. My life was so out of control that somehow those straight lines gave me a sense of false control. I'm sure many of you can identify with what I am saying.

Exercise was another biggie. Just like those straight lines in the carpet, running till I dropped provided a sense of momentary control. Running was also my escape. I could go far away in my head, at least for a while, and find a brief reprieve from the storm that always awaited me around the bend.

At the risk of sounding sacrilegious, prayer also served as a sort of Band-Aid. I certainly believe in the power of prayer. However, prayer alone will not change your situation or heal your heart. Prayer plus action is what will make the difference in your life. I spent hours praying in my walk-in closet, but it was not until I coupled my prayers with intentional action steps that I began to see change in my life. Notice I said *my* life, not Ben's. Although I prayed *a lot* for Ben, my prayers could never override his free will. But I am firmly convinced that my prayers for myself gave me the strength and the perseverance to walk my personal healing journey. Prayer does work. We must accept, however, that prayer is not a magic wand. Even God Himself allows all people, abusers and victims alike, to make choices throughout their lives.

While prayer was vital to sustaining me in many ways, my most significant Band-Aid was mothering. I *loved* raising my kids, but what was meant to be a role became a hideout in my life. Mothering was more than what I did; it became in large part who I was. It became the identity I hung on to for many years with white knuckles. I focused so intently on my kids, hoping the pain would go away, but doing so also proved not to be enough to adequately and permanently treat the trauma. Throwing birthday parties, hosting sleepovers, and baking apple pies for them still remain as wonderful memories. However, none of those special moments stopped the abuse in our home, and none of those memories were able to bring me to where I am today. Warm memories can bring a smile to our faces, but they won't ever bring healing to our hearts.

I have mentioned just a few of the Band-Aids I used in an effort to manage the incessant pain I felt inside. While none of them were inherently bad, all were fruitless attempts to anesthetize my pain. In the end, they caused me more pain because they didn't work.

Two decades of working with hurting people in private practice have shown me just how reluctant we can be to face our emotional wounds. Often people misuse drugs, food, sex, relationships, work, and even exercise to avoid feeling the pain that lies right beneath the surface. There is a direct correlation between their self-sabotaging behaviors and their wounds. Sadly, many people don't recognize that unaddressed emotional pain is driving their decisions.

"For me, I found myself going deeper and deeper into the bottle trying to numb my pain," Sara shared during a recent counseling session. "Alcohol seemed like the perfect escape because drinking, at least initially, appeared to affect only me and no one else. But as I have made the commitment to dig deeper, I've come to realize that alcohol fixes nothing. It is a temporary Band-Aid with no real power to heal my hurt."

The Irrevocable Band-Aid

So far, we have talked about various types of metaphorical Band-Aids that we use to try to mitigate our emotional pain. None of these Band-Aids, used for the purposes of numbing our pain or distracting ourselves from the pain, actually prove useful. If anything, in the long run, we feel worse.

There is one, however, that deserves special attention and focus: suicide. One out of every five women who are the victims of domestic violence attempt suicide. Their depression and overall sense of hopelessness can reach overwhelming proportions. Many victims feel trapped. Some are actually trapped, knowing that any attempt to leave could result in their death and/or the deaths of their children. This is a very real danger that necessitates the need for a well-thought-out safety plan and the support of outsiders such as police, a counselor, and/or well-informed family members and friends (see appendix B for safety plans).

Suicide can appear to be a victim's only answer. I intentionally used the word *appear*. When you're so deep in the miry pit of abuse, suicide can feel like the only way out, but it's not. It is an irrevocable Band-Aid that can never be reversed. Suicide is a permanent conclusion to your life, while healing well can be a permanent victory in your life. When a person chooses suicide, they permanently close the door to any other options. The information presented in these pages is the absolute antithesis to that choice. The message of healing well and living free was birthed out of my very real agony, with the hope that you will also choose a free and healthy life for yourself.

I get it. I truly do. For many years during my marriage to Ben, I had to push away temptations to end my life. Many times while driving down the freeway, I wanted to drive over a cliff's edge or into a wall. Other times I thought about ingesting an entire bottle of pills. Anything to stop the pain that was so intense and relentless. These thoughts terrified me.

This is the first time (as I type this chapter) I have shared my struggle with suicidal thoughts during that time in my life. So if you're a counselor reading this book, *please* ask your clients if they are struggling with the decision to end their pain too. No one ever asked me, and I never told.

My deep love for and commitment to my children kept me from following through on this irrevocable decision. I could never do something like that to them. Today I understand that it was not only my love for my children but also the embers of love for myself, though barely flickering, that kept me from that tragic decision. I also see how Jesus held me during those times even though I couldn't feel Him or see Him. He was there. Likewise, He is with you too.

If you are struggling with thoughts of taking your life, please reach out for help by calling the National Suicide Prevention Lifeline at 1-800-273-8255 or dialing 911 for an immediate response.

Time Does Not Heal All Wounds

Unaddressed emotional pain doesn't heal with time. Time does not heal all wounds. Time simply distances us from the injury; it never cures the ailment. You cannot heal from what you will not feel, and you cannot feel what you will not talk about. In order to heal, we have to feel, and in order to feel, we have to share our story. Sharing your story with a trusted and trained counselor is an integral part of healing well. It's in the sharing that we begin to allow ourselves to feel the emotions associated with that injury (or injuries). Feeling is the precursor to healing.

In chapter 3, I explained how permitting ourselves to grieve is part of the process of healing well. Grieving is not a Band-Aid. Grieving is to emotional injury as effectively cleaning the wound is to physical injury. The point is there are no shortcuts to healing well. Shortcuts rob us of the opportunity to integrate all our life experiences: the good, the bad, the unconscionable. Who we are and who we are becoming, is the result of where we've been and what we have experienced.

The residual effects of abuse are an ugly truth. If it's your truth, as it was mine, you may want to run from it, thinking that if you run hard enough and long enough, it won't catch up to you. But it will. The pain abuse causes demands to be faced, felt, and properly fixed. Listen to your pain. It's a powerful teacher.

Questions to Ponder

1. Looking at your life, how have you avoided feeling your emotional pain? Have you been tempted to take shortcuts with the hope of somehow "getting over it" or that "time heals all wounds"?

2. What are some of the Band-Aids you've used in an attempt to numb your pain or avoid it altogether? How effective have they truly been?

3. What do you think would or could happen if you permitted yourself to feel the emotions that are tied to your wounds?

4. Are you at a place in your life where you are willing to listen to your pain? If so, what is it telling you?

   (It is important that you discern between what your pain is trying to communicate to you and the faulty messages or outright lies your abuser said to you or about you. If you are struggling to differentiate between the two, discuss this with your counselor or a trusted friend.)

5. Have thoughts of suicide ever crossed your mind? Do you recognize the fact that suicide permanently terminates your access to a free life?

   (When I was at my lowest points, this option seemed viable. At that time, I never pictured I would be where I am today. I understand that it seems as if your life may never change for the better. But that's not true. It can and it will if you stay the course. Tell someone you trust that you need help, support, and resources to combat these self-harming thoughts. Or reach out for help by calling the National Suicide Prevention Lifeline at 1-800-273-8255 or dialing 911 for an immediate response.)

6. What are some specific ways in which you can positively respond to your emotional pain that will provide genuine and authentic healing rather than a momentary reprieve?

Below is a list of positive ways to respond to your pain. Mark the ones you are currently doing. If there are certain ones you are avoiding, discuss them with your counselor or a trusted friend. What do you believe may be inhibiting you? (This is another opportunity to look at faulty thinking.)

☐ I have started writing my story.

☐ I have broken the silence by sharing my story with a trusted friend or counselor.

☐ I am learning to call what I've experienced abuse.

☐ I am no longer minimizing, justifying, or rationalizing what has been done to me.

☐ I am no longer making excuses or taking responsibility for my abuser's abusive choices and actions.

☐ I have allowed myself to begin the grieving process.

☐ I recognize the cycle of abuse and accept that my trying harder will not stop it.

☐ I am beginning to recognize the effects of abuse and the symptoms of PTSD.

☐ I am willing to pursue professional help for a proper diagnosis in the event that I may be suffering from PTSD.

☐ I am beginning to identify the Band-Aids I have attempted to use to numb or avoid my pain.

Prayer of Reflection

Jesus, I want to heal well. So often it feels like too much to bear, and I just want to give up. I am tired. So very, very tired. I am tired of trying to make this relationship work. I am tired of waiting for him to change. My heart is heavy, and my body is exhausted. The idea of letting time heal all wounds is enticing. But I know it doesn't work. I have tried a variety of ways to numb and ignore my pain. Yet the pain is still there. Band-Aids don't heal broken arms, and they certainly can't heal broken hearts. Help me not to give in to the temptation of giving up on myself or giving up on the opportunity to heal well. Through You, true healing is possible. When my faulty thinking clouds truth, gently draw me back to the good path You have designed for me. Amen.

God's Enduring Promises

He heals the brokenhearted, binding up their wounds. (Psalm 147:3 TLB)

Be strong and of good courage, do not fear nor be afraid of them; for the LORD your God, He is the One who goes with you. He will not leave you nor forsake you. (Deuteronomy 31:6 NKJV)

> The LORD is my rock, my fortress, and my savior;
> my God is my rock, in whom I find protection.
> He is my shield, the power that saves me,
> and my place of safety.
> I called on the LORD, who is worthy of praise,
> and he saved me from my enemies. (Psalm 18:2–3 NLT)

> The LORD is my rock, my fortress, and the One who
> rescues me;
> My God, my rock and strength in whom I trust and take
> refuge;
> My shield, and the horn of my salvation, my high tower—
> my stronghold.
> I call upon the LORD, who is worthy to be praised;
> And I am saved from my enemies. (Psalm 18:2–3 AMP)

6

I Tried So Hard
and Got So Little

Remember those beautiful summer days as a kid building sand castles along the seashore? Even if your childhood memories don't include trips to the beach, I'm sure you can picture this in your mind. You set out to build the biggest fortress, using various size buckets. You made countless trips back and forth to fill your little bucket with wet sand. The final touch was when you dug the moat to encircle your castle. Voila! You were ready to move in!

As children, we believed that if we dug the moat deep enough and built the castle big enough, it would be protected from the impending tide and all would be well. Right? But it didn't take long for high tide to close in and wash our masterpiece away. Some of us, determined to beat the waves, would try all the harder, filling our sand bucket at a rapid rate and rebuilding each part of the castle as it washed out to sea.

Like the little child who tries to keep the tide from sweeping her castle away, a woman in an abusive relationship often tries endlessly to stop the cycle of abuse. She hopes her abuser will change his behavior if she changes hers. She inadvertently accepts responsibility for her abuser's actions by believing that "If only I would have . . ." or "If only I hadn't . . ." she could have diffused the situation and prevented the explosion phase from happening.

As adults, we know that sand castles never last. The tide always wins. And just as a sand castle cannot withstand the force of the tide, your efforts cannot stop the cycle of abuse. An abusive partner will only change if he wants to. And statistically speaking, that is a highly unlikely outcome.

Abuse Is *Not* a Couple's Issue

Your efforts to stop the abuse will never work. Remember, abuse is not a couple's issue. If it were, then you could help to stop it. Since it's not, the most effective thing you can do is to focus on yourself. By focusing on yourself, I mean objectively separating what you can control from what you can't, then shifting your energy and focus away from your partner's actions (what you can't control) and toward yourself (what you can control).

I have spent numerous hours hovering around this very issue with some of my clients. I share with them exactly what I am saying to you now, and many of them politely nod as if to say, "I agree with you, Dr. Ramona, but I don't entirely believe you." Their response makes sense to me. We want to believe that our efforts to effect change will make a difference for the better in our relationships. The snag is that change requires both people to be pulling in the same direction.

Imagine sitting in a rowboat with your partner. You pick up your oar and vigorously begin paddling. All the while he sits there and stares at you or even perhaps attempts to pull the oar from your hands. What happens when only one person has their oar in the water, regardless of how intensely they paddle? The boat goes in circles! Sound familiar?

The "Oz" behind Abuse . . . Payoff!

In chapter 3, we talked about the mind-set of an abuser. Remember there is a payoff to the abuser for his behavior. This can be a tough concept to understand. Let me give you an illustration.

Money (more accurately, the management of money) was a constant stressor between Ben and me. He would want to spend money on items we clearly could not afford, placing us in deeper debt or behind on our bills. This caused me massive stress. But if I did not acquiesce to Ben's insistence that buying another (fill in the blank) was no big deal, I'd suffer the consequences. If he sensed that ignoring me wasn't working, he would escalate, often going from verbal assaults to physical ones.

Early in our marriage, I discovered that Ben had not paid our electric bill when we received a shut-off notice in the mail. Shortly after that, I found a receipt hidden under the couch. I asked Ben why he had chosen to buy another gun instead of paying our electric bill. In response, he picked me up and threw me against the headboard of our bed. In the future, I thought twice before questioning him about his spending. I reasoned that doing so simply was not worth the risk of experiencing his assaults against me. In many ways, it was easier just to give him what he wanted. Ben's abusive outbursts provided him with an advantage. I was scared to cross him. Hence, I either shut up or backed down. His abusive behavior clearly had a payoff.

For those of you who have not experienced physical assault like this in your relationship, please do not minimize your situation. Abuse of any kind is wrong, never excusable, and there's always a payoff for the abuser.

One particular client of mine endured years of verbal and emotional abuse. Her partner never physically assaulted her, but the toll the verbal and emotional abuse took on her was just as damaging. She described herself feeling frozen whenever her partner berated and verbally attacked her, often shutting down, unable to pull herself out of it. She too suffered from post-traumatic stress disorder, for which she wisely sought counseling to address the ongoing symptoms she was battling.

Regardless of how it is expressed, abuse is scary. It causes you to question yourself. It lies to you. The lie is that somehow the abuse is your fault. Somehow you caused it. Somehow you could have prevented it. An abuser loves to capitalize on this lie. He negates his responsibility by making his victim the reason or the cause for his abusive behavior. As we discussed in chapter 3, abusive behavior is fueled by a mind-set that includes both entitlement and lack of empathy. An abuser believes he is entitled to say and do the things he says and does. When they result in a verbal, emotional, sexual, or physical outburst, then it's his victim's fault.

The fact is you are not responsible for the abuse. However, certain *positive* qualities you possess make you more vulnerable to tolerating an abusive partner and remaining with him. How could it be that your positive qualities set you up to stay in an abusive relationship? Let me explain.

A Nicer You Doesn't Make for a Nicer Him

Her name is Sandra L. Brown. She is the author and researcher who taught me how certain positive attributes I had in excess actually kept the cycle of abuse spinning. In her excellent book *Women Who Love Psychopaths*, Brown educates women regarding something she calls "super-traits." Super-traits, simply put, are qualities a woman may have in excess that translate into risk factors when unrecognized. They include high loyalty, high tolerance, excessive empathy, trusting (before it is earned), and the ability to invest heavily in a relationship (even at her own expense). These attributes will likely not cause her harm in emotionally healthy relationships with family members and friends. But these very same qualities that are appreciated by others will be used by an abuser to manipulate and entrap her, sometimes for years and perhaps even a lifetime. These traits are admirable when in proper balance, but they become risk factors when applied disproportionately to "fix" an abusive relationship.

We can all agree that the above traits are valuable and good. What Brown discovered, though, is that women who possess such qualities in excess—when others might have them in moderation—are more vulnerable to men who are likely to abuse. Consider, if you will, if you have ever been told you are especially loyal. Especially tolerant. Especially empathetic. Especially trusting. Perhaps you have compared yourself to others and wondered why they didn't seem to have these qualities in as much abundance as you do. Now note how an abusive man might use these qualities to his advantage, given that he feels (1) entitled and (2) a lack of empathy toward you.

It's a recipe for abuse. Toward you.

Granting more empathy, increased tolerance, continued loyalty, undeserved trust, and an overinvestment into the relationship will *never* cause him to change. Doing so will only leave you exhausted, despondent, and stuck riding the crazy train of an abusive relationship. Getting off this train requires that you realize you are on it as well as the part you play in keeping it going (your super-traits). Until you understand the significance of these super-traits, you will continue to try harder and end up with little to nothing, except pain.

Understanding how my super-traits were being used against me was a major paradigm shift in my healing well journey. I wasted so much energy minimizing Ben's abusive behavior (tolerance), keeping the secret (loyalty), and vigorously attempting to understand why he would hurt me when he said he loved me (empathy). At last, I understood that trying harder was never going to stop the abuse. I finally realized that I needed to shift the use of these traits away from him and my attempts to save the marriage and direct them instead toward saving myself and my children. Yet the feeling I experienced after this realization was surprising.

Although I had shared my story, broken the silence, learned about the cycle of abuse, and identified both his mind-set and my own super-traits, I felt . . . shame. Where did this come from?

Shame: A Toxic Foe

Shame is a nasty demon. In my opinion, it's probably one of the nastiest. What I have discovered through my years working in private practice is that shame is at the root of every destructive behavior, thought pattern, and self-sabotaging cycle.

There is a huge difference between shame and guilt. Guilt is an appropriate and necessary emotion when you know you have done something wrong or hurtful to another person. Guilt says what you did was bad. But shame says *you* are bad. Guilt is about the behavior. Shame is about the person—it's an assault on your identity. Guilt can be the precursor to change if you respond appropriately with a sincere apology and a desire to correct your behavior or attitude. Guilt can actually foster hope when you respond in a healthy fashion. Shame, on the other hand, leaves you feeling despondent and entrapped and very often repeating the very thing that is causing you and others pain. We see this phenomenon in people struggling with addiction. They use, they feel shame for using, they promise never to use again, then they end up using again to drown out the shame. This self-sabotaging behavior will continue over and over until they realize the deception of shame. No true change ever results from shame. When the focus of your negative thoughts constantly reminds you of how awful you are, you can be pretty certain that shame is the catalyst driving those thoughts. Since your abuser's behavior is his choice and not your fault, shame is never warranted and never helpful. So why did I struggle with it for so many years, and why do you?

My shame was birthed out of feeling like a failure. Regardless of how hard I tried or what I did, nothing changed. Then when I made the decision to focus on myself and my kids, I felt like I was giving up—on Ben, us, our marriage, and our family. I knew I was not a person who gave up, yet that's exactly what it felt like.

When you make the decision to focus on you and your kids, you are not deserting your positive traits; rather, you are deploying them where they can actually make a difference. Shame wants to blind you to this fact. Shame wants to make you feel as if you are being disloyal when really you are being loyal to yourself and your kids. You are not being uncaring; rather, you are caring for yourself and your kids. This realignment of the recipient of your positive actions is what you need to focus on.

It was a mind-bender for me to imagine that all my efforts in remaining loyal, empathetic, tolerant, and hugely invested in our relationship weren't working. Actually, the harder I tried, the worse Ben got. Yet for many years, I believed I was failing miserably. Finally, I began to see that my efforts to stop the cycle could only be effective if they were *not* directed toward Ben. The only way to stop the cycle was to shift my focus. This felt like I was turning my back on Ben and everything it meant to be a "loyal, loving, Christian wife," but I've come to realize it wasn't. Those faulty beliefs were fueled by shame, and shame does not go away simply because we've identified it. Shame must be replaced with truth. Truth is the antidote to shame.

In the next chapter, we'll discuss the extraordinary impact that taking responsibility has in a victim's life. There are definitely areas in your life and in your thinking that need to be addressed. But until you are able to identify how shame is keeping you stuck, you will be unable to move forward toward healthier thinking, which will result in healthier choices.

Minimizing Your Pain, Your Reality, Yourself

In order for shame to keep a victim in the destructive cycle of abuse, she must, in some way, minimize her pain. Otherwise she literally wouldn't be able to function. Our bodies demand we pay attention to stress and emotional pain.

I had internalized the stress for so long that eventually my bottled-up emotions started to find their way out through the lining of my stomach! A painful ulcer was demanding that I listen to my gut, both literally and figuratively. I later developed an autoimmune disease. Years of unchecked and ignored stress can take its toll on your body, too. I'm not a medical doctor, but I have personal experience with what can happen when we minimize our pain.

I was diagnosed with rheumatoid arthritis when I was twenty-nine years old. To this day, I believe that this disease resulted primarily from the constant stress of living in an abusive relationship and trying with all my might to make it work. I am not going to go into the details of my disease, but I am definitely a walking miracle. The diagnosis scared me to the point that I took some drastic measures to regain my health (although leaving Ben was not one of them). I worked hand in hand with an excellent naturopathic physician for over two years and did absolutely everything he instructed me to do. For the first time in my life, I really listened to my pain. And thank God, I did. I am well today. It was a miracle indeed. I shudder to think how things would have turned out if I had not finally listened. Please listen. Ignoring your pain can come with a very high price. Don't ignore it!

If I Try Just One More Time

In my opinion, the granddaddy mantra of rationalization that keeps the cycle of abuse spinning is "If I try just one more time." Just one more time *always* begets another "one more time." Until you say, "Enough!" you will automatically default to this erroneous belief again and again and again. The rationale, as faulty as it is, implies that if you (and notice the pronoun *you*) try just one more time, then this time things will be different. This time he will understand how his behavior is breaking your heart. This time he will finally change. The truth is that this time never comes. Because, and it bears repeating until you fully believe it, you cannot change him regardless of how hard you try. The sooner you accept this truth, the sooner you can get off the crazy train. Just like any train, this one also stops at various depots. I can safely assume there have been many times you have considered getting off the train, and you may have even gotten off for a while. The goal is never to get back on it.

My desire is that you will fully understand that doing the following things will *never* result in an abuse-free life with your partner:

- Minimizing your pain
- Rationalizing that he will stop the abuse because of your loyalty, empathy, tolerance, and continued investment in the relationship
- Believing the abuse will stop if you try just one more time

Doing these things only results in more shame when the cycle inevitably repeats itself. Until you recognize and accept this, the cycle of abuse will not stop. This is the part you play in keeping the cycle going. When you stop minimizing your pain, rationalizing his abusive behavior, and shaming yourself when your efforts to help him change don't work, then you will start to notice a change in the cycle. His old antics will slowly begin to lose the power and pull they once had over you.

The change you're yearning for will happen in *you*, but only after you make a shift away from him and toward yourself. An enormous part of healing well involves this shift and a pursuit of healthy emotional self-care.

That's why you are reading this book. The nuggets tucked inside each chapter have the ability to change your life for the better, but you must choose to believe. Believe that your life can be different. Believe that you are worth being treated with gentleness, respect, and kindness. True love is safe love. True love protects its beloved. True love never involves fear. Until you recognize the self-destructive nature of shame, the cost involved in minimizing your pain, and the lie behind trying just one more time, you will remain in the pain. It's not worth it.

Do you believe this? If yes, I am ecstatically relieved for you. If not yet, then recall my words to you in the introduction: until you can believe for yourself, "believe in my belief." I believe you can change. I believe you can learn to heal well. I believe you are worth it.

Questions to Ponder

1. Now that you understand super-traits, can you identify any of these qualities within yourself (high tolerance, high empathy, extreme loyalty, etc.)? Do you understand how these very same traits need to be redirected toward yourself and healing well? How do you intend to apply each of these traits to yourself?

2. At this point in your healing journey, can you observe the impact shame has had on you? Describe what that has looked like in your life.

3. Trying harder does not stop the abusive cycle. What other faulty beliefs have you embraced that you now realize were lies all along?

4. How have you minimized your pain? What are some of the consequences you have experienced as a result of ignoring your pain?

5. Do you believe that trying just one more time will never result in your desire for change or bring an end to the abuse? If yes, explain why. If no, why not?

Prayer of Reflection

God, I am beginning to recognize faulty thinking that has kept me in bondage for a long time. I really believed that if I tried harder, prayed more, and believed enough, then he would change, and the abuse would stop. The fact that the abuse has not stopped, and has even gotten worse in many ways, has confused me. Certainly, I know how hard I have tried. And yet the only things I really have to show for it are exhaustion and despondency. Admittedly, I have really struggled with feeling angry with You too. At times even now, my faith falters, and I am tempted to give up. Being able to admit my feelings with You and toward You is liberating. I trust that because You understand me, You do not hold any of this against me. Your love for me is not based on what I do but on who You are. You do love me, and I thank You for loving me unconditionally. Help me to accept Your love and to trust in You when I cannot see the way. I did try so hard and got so little. Help me to believe that my pain is not wasted and that You intend to use it for good in my life. Help me to learn to truly love myself as You love me. Amen.

God's Enduring Promises

"Not by might nor by power, but by my Spirit," says the LORD Almighty. (Zechariah 4:6)

> Instead of your shame
>> you will receive a double portion,
> and instead of disgrace
>> you will rejoice in your inheritance.
> And so you will inherit a double portion in your land,
>> and everlasting joy will be yours. (Isaiah 61:7)

But as for me, I trust [confidently] in You and Your
      greatness, O LORD;
I said, "You are my God."
My times are in Your hands;
Rescue me from the hand of my enemies and from those
      who pursue and persecute me. (Psalm 31:14–15 AMP)

Trust in the LORD and do good;
    dwell in the land and enjoy safe pasture.
Take delight in the LORD,
    and he will give you the desires of your heart.
Commit your way to the LORD;
    trust in him and he will do this:
He will make your righteous reward shine like the dawn,
    your vindication like the noonday sun.
Be still before the LORD
    and wait patiently for him;
do not fret when people succeed in their ways,
    when they carry out their wicked schemes.
      (Psalm 37:3–7)

7

Take an Honest Look at Yourself, Your Life, and Your Choices

Victims of any form of abuse tend to blame themselves. I have observed this very sad phenomenon many times when working with victims of sexual abuse. Even small children who are victimized by sexual predators often believe they somehow caused it. Statistically speaking, sexual abuse perpetrators are typically known by the child, which further exacerbates the ugliness of this kind of trauma and betrayal. As adults, we recognize the ridiculous logic here. There is no way a child could somehow be responsible for such an atrocious offense.

Healthy Acceptance of Your Own Limitations

Your stomach probably churned when you considered the injustice of the previous example. But such is also the case with domestic violence. The victims also know the perpetrators, and many, like childhood victims of sexual abuse, blame themselves or take on responsibility that belongs to the abusers. Most often, these relationships started off like a storybook romance. The victims were wooed and convinced they were in a story that would end well for them.

Abusers tend to be incredibly charming, which is the flip side of super manipulative. This fact is very important to recognize. You didn't just run off into the sunset with this guy. He wooed you, enamored you, and in most cases, swept you off your feet. If you recall, my Prince Charming (and it's interesting he's called "Charming") looked like he stepped out of a Hollywood movie. He was witty, polite to my parents, let my two younger brothers chum around with us, and took me on many whimsical dates and trips to places I hadn't seen. We even attended a ball! Yes, I said a ball. I was Cinderella, or so I thought. However, the Cinderella I read about didn't end up with black eyes and choke marks around her neck.

So when Cinderella realizes she is actually the lead role in her own horror film rather than a fairy tale, she may attempt to reach out and share a morsel of her story with someone she hopes will understand her. Unfortunately, the very first question most victims of domestic violence hear when they finally muster up the courage to speak is, "Why don't you just leave him?" This question, often asked by well-intentioned people who have absolutely no clue how complicated these relationships can be, typically incites tremendous shame, confusion, and self-blame in the heart of the victim. Clearly, it implies, "What's wrong with you?" The judgment is evident in the asking of the question, even if the person is not intending to judge. You may even find yourself wondering, *That's right. Why don't I leave him? Why do I keep going back only to be hurt once again?* The answer is not simple, nor is it a one-size-fits-all explanation. Women return to these relationships for many reasons. In chapter 9, I will tackle this question. But for now, let's focus on you.

Now what? Now you know he's no Prince Charming, although the honeymoon phase in the cycle you are in may confuse you at times. You must repeatedly remind yourself that you are in a cycle. The theory behind the cycle of abuse has stood the test of time. Many researchers and domestic violence survivors attest to its validity. Believing it applies to you can take time. But you wouldn't be reading this book if you weren't ready to call it what it is. Now is all you have. This moment. Today. Right now. Taking an honest look at yourself, your life, and your choices is liberating, empowering, and at the heart of healing well.

Recall the research of Sandra L. Brown and how she demonstrated that victims of domestic violence have an excess of virtuous qualities—super-traits—such as high loyalty, high tolerance, excessive empathy, trusting people before they earn it, and continuing to invest in a harmful relationship when most would walk away. These excessive traits can become risk factors when not recognized. In my practice, I've seen time and again that domestic violence victims demonstrate an overabundance of personal responsibility as well.

During one of our counseling sessions with our pastor, he paused in the middle of his thought and said to Ben and me, "Bottom line, Ramona, you do too much, and Ben, you do too little. Ramona needs to stop overfunctioning, and Ben needs to step it up." At that point in our marriage, I was not even close to calling it abuse, breaking the silence, or doing anything I'm teaching you in this book. At that time, I did not disclose to our pastor what was really going on in our relationship. Hence, that was the reason why I thought couple's counseling was the solution. Nevertheless, this dear pastor of ours still spotted a very common occurrence in abusive relationships. The victim goes above and beyond, and the abuser expects it.

A little side note: After one particular incident in which Ben gave me a black eye, I was scheduled to meet with this pastor for an individual counseling session. I showed up wearing sunglasses and thick makeup around my bruised eye. I wanted to keep the sunglasses on during our session, so I said I had a headache and the lights bothered me. He asked me to remove my glasses. When he saw the obviously camouflaged eye, he said he wanted to call the police immediately. I begged him not to, stating, "If it ever happens again, I'll call the police." He reluctantly agreed. He told me if he ever saw me like that again he would not ask my permission but would call the authorities on the spot. My response? That was the last time I met with him for counseling. I continued hiding.

Self-Blame: A Detour through Quicksand

In order to take an honest look at yourself, you must first acknowledge this truth: you are not responsible for the abuse you have suffered. The blame you have been carrying around is not reflective of reality. As long as you continue to blame yourself for things you did not cause, you cannot control, and you cannot cure, you will carry the weight of this blame and feel stuck. Blame is the sibling of shame. Remember shame? Shame will keep you stuck. So will blame. Blame is the faulty logic that convinces you that you are playing a part in causing this pain to yourself, and if you are playing a part, then you must have some control or influence over what is happening to you. It's worth me repeating the mantra: abuse is not a couple's issue! It is not a communication problem! It is not about conflict resolution! An abuser's behavior is his choice. And he will continue to abuse you as long as you think you have the power to help him change.

Accepting your limitations is a healthy response and is actually the remedy to self-blame. No amount of empathy, tolerance, loyalty, believing the best, patience, or prayer is going to bring about the results you believed it would. It's not your fault. You are not responsible for him. You are responsible only for yourself and your children. You must begin to direct your super-traits toward yourself. Loving yourself is loving your kids. You and they deserve better. Your kids cannot make this choice for you. They are counting on you to say, "Enough!" This statement is not intended to heap guilt on you. Instead, it is intended to put the focus where it belongs: on saving yourself and your children, not your marriage or your relationship. And if you do not have children, you are still worth saving. Your life matters. You matter. Now, today, in this very moment, decide to show empathy, tolerance, and loyalty to yourself. Loving yourself is how you will heal from this. Choose to love yourself. No one can choose you but you.

One client tells the story of how a simple word picture helped her overcome shame and move into positive action. "I was sitting in the lobby of the courthouse, feeling such incredible guilt and shame. My back was literally bent with it. I was crying snotty tears in front of complete strangers as I waited to go before the judge to get a restraining order. I sent a quick text to a dear friend hundreds of miles away asking her to pray. She sent back a text that said, 'You're a momma bear. Your cubs need you. Roar!' That image somehow gave me courage. I dried my eyes and went before the judge and got that restraining order. That simple image really turned my thoughts around."

U-Turns Aren't Wrong Turns

If I asked you to share with me what your dreams and aspirations were prior to this relationship, could you tell me? Have you achieved them? If not, why not? It's obviously a rhetorical question. You know how they say you can't think about two things at the same time? Try it. Think about a fond memory you have of a close friend. Now think about when your favorite pet died (if you didn't have one, substitute another loss). Okay, now think about both of these things at the same time. You can't do it, right? In the same way, it's impossible to direct the majority or perhaps all of your energy toward making a toxic, abusive relationship work and at the same time pursue your hopes, goals, and dreams. One of them is going to dominate. It will always be your abuser, his needs, and keeping him happy. In essence, attempting to keep the peace requires you to put your desires on a back burner.

What made you come alive prior to all of this? What were some of the dreams and desires you had for your life before getting into this relationship? Sit for a moment and allow yourself to recall those dreams from days gone by. Which ones bring a smile to your face? Which ones perhaps bring a tear to your eye? Reconnecting with your dreams and the desires you held for your life is paramount to healing well, and it's a must to living free. I believe if our goals, dreams, and aspirations don't spark something energizing inside us, we're either dreaming someone else's dreams or trying to force ourselves to be someone or do something that just doesn't fit. This relationship, and all the focus and energy it demanded, got you off course. But like anytime you discover you've made a wrong turn, you can stop, reposition yourself, and make a U-turn. *You*-turns in life are sometimes necessary. They can be healthy choices that get you back on the road to pursuing your dreams.

"Mirror, Mirror on the Wall, Who Have I Become After All?"

As time passes, you may look back and wonder how you drifted so far away from your own dreams and passions. I can testify to this for sure. I'll never forget the day I looked at myself in the mirror and didn't recognize who was staring back at me. I had slowly metamorphosed into what is referred to as a "pseudo-self," or a false self. If our minds were not created to think two opposing thoughts simultaneously, what makes us think we can live two opposing lives simultaneously and not pay the price for it? My public persona could have fooled even the most astute observer. I graduated valedictorian of my undergraduate class, managed to keep my figure after having three babies and gaining 111 pounds with my last child (I did a lot of sit-ups and ran like a hamster on a wheel!), went on to obtain my master's degree, and graduated as "Community Counseling Student of the Year." I codirected a counseling facility for seven years while housing anywhere from two to eight professional and semiprofessional skateboarders in our home. I became a master secret bearer. My public self fooled everyone. My private self was a whole different story.

Notice I was a counselor. A counselor! Abuse can find its way into any race, religion, occupation, or socioeconomic class. Abusers strut in fancy suits, perform open-heart surgeries, drive tractors, give speeding tickets, wear NFL jerseys, and preach sermons. And victims also come in every size, shape, and color. I became a counselor because I wanted to help people. What I eventually realized is that you can't help anyone until you help yourself. You can't give away what you don't have. By God's grace, this truth really started to sink into my brain prior to me getting my PsyD. However, several years before I pursued my doctorate, I was in private practice. I remember the exact day I walked into my colleague's office and said I was stepping away from the counseling profession. Her jaw dropped! For all intents and purposes, I had a very lucrative counseling practice. But I could no longer live an incongruent life.

I encouraged my clients to embrace truth in their lives. Truth is where we heal. Doing so worked for my clients. The incongruence between what I said and how I was living became too much for me to bear. After making the tough but wise decision to step away from private practice, I referred my clients to reputable colleagues who would continue supporting them in their treatment needs. For me, I needed to find truth again. My public and private selves needed to match. I desired to connect with my passions again, to figure out who I was, how I had gotten here, and where I wanted to go. This was definitely not an overnight transformation. It actually took three counselors, one support group (that I completed twice), and several years of intentionally committing to healing well to find my inner congruency again. I am so very grateful that the discomfort of living a lie—presenting one way to the public and another way in private—became too much for me to continue masquerading. It's crucial that you really think about how much you've changed. If outsiders could take a peek behind the curtain of your private life, what would they see? Your goals, your dreams, your purpose in life did not change simply because you did. They are still fully intact waiting for you to pursue them again. Will you?

All of this can be summed up in your choices. If you do not choose to continue on the path of healing well by recognizing the destructiveness of self-blame, the cost of directing your energy to maintain an abusive relationship, the price you are paying to keep the secret, and the toll all of this is taking on you, then the real you will continue to fade away. Who do you see when you look in the mirror? This time let the *true* you answer the question. She's in there. Listen to her.

Questions to Ponder

1. Can you see how blaming yourself for your abuser's behavior has taken its toll on you?
2. Taking responsibility for yourself, your life, and your choices is empowering. But only you can do this. What is still keeping you from choosing you?
3. When you look in the mirror, who do you see? How have you changed? Are those closest to you noticing the impact the abuse is having on you?
4. List the goals, dreams, and passions you once held dear. Are you ready to pursue them again? Who and what can support you in reconnecting with your dreams? Consider, if you

haven't already, working with a trained domestic violence counselor and joining a support group for victims of domestic violence.

Prayer of Reflection

Jesus, it is painful to see how much I have changed. When I look in the mirror, the woman looking back at me isn't the me I once knew. It's hard to admit this, but it's true. Living in this toxic relationship and keeping the secret have taken their toll on me. So much effort is needed now for me to complete even the most menial of tasks. I wear a mask, and I hide behind it. Help me, Jesus, to remove the mask and to see myself as You do with a future and a hope. I know that all things are possible for those who believe. Enable me to believe where I still have so much doubt in myself and in my future. I want to dream again and pursue the aspirations I held before this relationship became my focus. Open my eyes and open my heart to the wonderful possibilities that await me. I want to reconnect with all the things that used to inspire me and fill me with joy. I want to believe that there is life again after abuse. Show me the way. Amen.

God's Enduring Promises

But those who wait for the LORD [who expect, look for,
    and hope in Him]
Will gain new strength and renew their power;
They will lift up their wings [and rise up close to God] like
    eagles [rising toward the sun];
They will run and not become weary,
They will walk and not grow tired. (Isaiah 40:31 AMP)

I can do all things [which He has called me to do] through Him who strengthens and empowers me [to fulfill His purpose—I am self-sufficient in Christ's sufficiency; I am ready for anything and equal to anything through Him who infuses me with inner strength and confident peace.] (Philippians 4:13 AMP)

> Though I am surrounded by troubles,
>   you will protect me from the anger of my enemies.
> You reach out your hand,
>   and the power of your right hand saves me.
> The LORD will work out his plans for my life—
>   for your faithful love, O LORD, endures forever.
>   (Psalm 138:7–8 NLT)

He is close to all who call on him sincerely. He fulfills the desires of those who reverence and trust him; he hears their cries for help and rescues them. (Psalm 145:18–19 TLB)

8

Where Is God When I Hurt?

As a therapist, I have sat with people from all walks of life and listened to them share their stories of heartbreak and loss. Such people are despondent, sometimes desperate, and often have dwindling hope.

One of the most common questions victims of domestic violence ask is, "How did I end up here?" This makes sense, since nobody plans to get into an abusive relationship. And on the heels of that question, I often hear, "I tried so hard. I took him back so many times, believing this time the promise of change would last. When it didn't, I found myself questioning everything I believed to be true." And for many of us, this may include questioning God. Down deep we wonder, *Where is God? Is He aware of my pain? Does He even care?* These are fair questions, all of which I asked myself multiple times while living my own story, albeit with broken promises and an ending I did not want.

For some of you, your spiritual journey may be characterized by joy and comfort; others may have stories marked by disappointment and pain. If this chapter is too difficult for you to read in one sitting, please feel free to set it aside and come back to it when you feel ready. Even if you do not believe in God or adhere to a particular faith, I gently and respectfully encourage you to read this chapter.

To be honest, this was one of the most painful chapters of the book for me to write. I cried most of the way through it. I love Jesus very much, but I would be lying to you if I said I didn't struggle with the question of why God didn't seem to do anything about the suffering I was experiencing. It was almost like He was apathetic to my pain. Why would God allow me to suffer at the hands of a person I loved and trusted?

I found that understanding my faith story and being honest regarding my feelings about God helped me take the next step toward healing and wholeness.

My Faith Story

I took my first Communion when I was in the second grade. In Catholic families, a child's first communion can be as elaborate as a wedding. Little girls get to dress like princesses in frilly, white, miniature wedding dresses, complete with a veil. It is a big deal. And when children take their first Holy Communion, it is also the first time they go to confession. I remember standing with my fellow classmates in line. We were nervous and giggling and getting in trouble for not standing still. We were waiting to go into a little room to talk through a screen to a priest and confess our sins.

When it was my turn, I could see a man dressed in black peering at me through the screen. I was scared. I remember making up a sin that I hoped would appease the priest. "I was mean to my brother," I blurted out. It was basically true and the best thing I could come up with under duress. After I made my first confession, the priest gave me a list of things to do: say five Our Fathers, three Hail Marys, and you're golden (he didn't really say the "and you're golden" part!). As soon as I left the tiny confessional, I immediately dropped to my knees. I remember thinking that I'd better do what he said right away or God was going to lightning bolt me!

Every Friday at school, we attended Mass. I would look at the statues and the stained glass, and I always wanted to sit near the front row. There was a decorated box on the front altar, and I would stare at it intently. It contained the Eucharist, also referred to as the Holy Communion. I was taught that after the priest prayed over the Eucharist, it literally became Christ's body and blood, given for me.

Church felt holy and important, but I also felt as if God was in that type of holy box, somewhere just out of my reach. I am extremely grateful for the Catholic influence in my life, but it was not until my teenage years that I came to understand God in a more personal way.

When I was seventeen years old, God used several people in my life to show me that Jesus desired to have a relationship with me that went beyond my childhood religious customs.

As I shared earlier, my future husband Ben was the first person to speak to me directly about Jesus. Shortly after we met, he asked me, "What do you think about Jesus?" His question struck me as odd, like he was some sort of religious weirdo. Ben had recently become a Christian himself, and he liked to tell others about his faith.

A year later, I met Chelsey. I was attending public school for the first time my senior year of high school. We met while having our school physicals. She was trying out for cheerleading; I was participating in track. Chelsey asked me about the Lord in a very natural way. Our friendship not only helped me grow in faith but it has also stood the test of time. More than thirty years later, we are still best friends. She is one of those people with whom I can be completely honest, and whenever we talk, we end up speaking about the Lord and what He is doing in our lives.

I am so grateful for Chelsey. God used her gentle demeanor to help me understand that I could have a personal relationship with

Jesus Christ. She invited me to attend a Christian group called Student Venture. My dad was suspicious of my renewed interest in church and Christianity, thinking I had gotten involved with some sort of cult.

While my parents would later come to a saving knowledge of Jesus Christ themselves, my dad in particular was not pleased with my decision at the time. As a result of my newfound belief in Christ, my dad gave me the ultimatum to leave my faith or leave their house. Therefore, I spent most of my senior year living elsewhere. Initially, I lived out of my B-210 Datsun, and later I was able to stay with friends.

During that time, I met two wonderful sisters who were a few years older than me. They would prove to be lifelong friends and play an important role in my faith story. Over the next few months, we worked together as waitresses. They invited me to live with them, and I slept on a mattress in their dining room. They showed me what it meant to really love someone with God's love. They did not pass judgment. They did not speak religious jargon. They just showed compassion and cared about me when the chips were down in my life.

Up until that point, on the rare occasion that I heard the term *born again*, I didn't understand it and thought it sounded strange. One morning I was sitting at the breakfast table with another friend. She told me a story from the Bible about a guy named Nicodemus.

Nicodemus was from a religious crowd, so fearing his friends would shun him, he went to see Jesus at night. Jesus explained to him that the only way to enter the kingdom of God was to be born again. He asked Jesus what it meant to be born again. After all, reasoned Nicodemus, a mother can't give birth to the same child twice. But Jesus patiently explained to Nicodemus what it meant.

Being born again means to be born by the Spirit, which is believing that Jesus is the Son of God. As the story continues, the next sentence says, "For God so loved the world that he gave his one and only Son, that whoever believes in him shall not perish but have eternal life" (John 3:16).

That day, sitting at the breakfast table, I made the decision to accept Jesus as my Savior. I had been seeking a kind of love and security that I could count on and an acceptance that was not contingent on performance. I found all those things when I chose to believe in Jesus Christ.

One evening, shortly after graduating from high school, I saw a man named Richard Roberts speaking on television. While pointing at the camera, he said (and it felt as if he was speaking directly to me), "You are supposed to go to Oral Roberts University." There was an 800 number on the bottom of the TV screen, so I picked up the phone and dialed! Someone answered and told me all about the college. It seemed like the perfect fit. I immediately applied and was accepted.

Two weeks later, I had packed my things. My mom gave me $211 from her bathrobe pocket, and my dad gave me a crucifix. A very dear friend of mine flew out from back East to drive with me from California to Oklahoma. The whole event seems extraordinary now. I did not consider other schools. I just felt as if God wanted me to go, so I did.

Physically, my freshman year of college was very difficult. I had a herniated disc in my lower back that was getting progressively worse. Even though I did not have health insurance, I was able to have back surgery at the City of Faith Hospital at Oral Roberts University. They did not charge me a single dime for the surgery. To this day, I hold deep gratitude in my heart for the benevolence of that hospital. Throughout that school year, God used many people at the college to genuinely care for me and help me grow in my faith.

Between my freshman and sophomore years of college, I left Oral Roberts University to marry Ben. It would end up taking me seven years to finish my undergraduate degree. I continued going to school as we began a family. We also both worked, Ben as a night security guard and me as the assistant manager of the apartment complex in which we lived. Looking back, I can clearly see God's hand on my life as we had child number one, then number two, and finally the exclamation point to our family . . . number three!

Ben and I were very naïve in many ways, so "planning a family" was not on our radar, to say the least. If you can even believe it, I had the first baby during my spring break from school, the second baby during the first week of my summer break, and the final baby on the very last day of a Christmas break. No one could have planned that! God in His mercy was looking out for me, since clearly I was not.

They say it's best to marry someone who shares your faith, and Ben and I both believed in God. We talked about going to Bible school together, and our plan was to devote ourselves to full-time ministry. I believe we were sincere in our desire to serve the Lord. Yet in all that sincerity, I experienced the first of countless physical assaults at the hands of my alleged "Christian" husband while we both attended Bible school.

One minute he would be praying and studying the Bible, and the next moment his temper would spiral out of control. Of course, no one knew the ugly truth except me, Ben, and later our three precious children (a reality that still pains me to this day). At church, we appeared to be the perfect couple, but at home, things were becoming increasingly less than perfect.

Somehow we both managed to graduate, and I delivered the valedictorian speech to our graduating class. There is no way I could have done that apart from God's grace and mercy in my life. In the end, my ability to take a stand and leave the abusive relationship was in large part due to the confidence I acquired while pursuing my education. This growing confidence eventually helped me say, "Enough is enough!"

Believing in God did not mean I did not question Him as the abuse continued and escalated. I talked to God almost constantly about the mess of a marriage I was in. I would go for long walks, crying and talking to the Lord. In my utter desperation to see change, and after reading about the significance of anointing people with oil in the Bible, I remember getting olive oil from our pantry and tracing a small cross on Ben's body while he slept. I cried out to God, asking Him to change Ben's heart and save my marriage. I know this sounds nuts! But I was willing to try just about anything to elicit change.

You see, in my mind, I had done all the things I was supposed to do as a "good Christian wife." I had married someone who believed in God. I had prayed with him and for him. I had supported him through countless ups, downs, and near crises. But, in the end, all I ended up with were bruised eyes and a broken heart.

Nothing I did was making things better, and it seemed like my prayers were ineffective. (Looking back, I am reminded of David in the Psalms.) I recall one afternoon, about ten years into my marriage, when I was home alone. I was crying bitterly on our family room couch, screaming at the top of my lungs, "Where are you, God? Are You up there? Do You see me? Do You care?" In my total despondency, I asked God if He was on a coffee break! Surely, He could see how my husband treated me. Why did He seem so silent and so very far away? It didn't make any sense.

Today, I have come to realize that I could have prayed until Jesus came back and my former spouse was not going to change. An abuser's decision to change is not going to result from you praying more, having more faith, believing more, or any of the other things I've mentioned. I have repeated this truth several times so far. Do you believe it yet?

The true miracle, in my opinion, is when you begin to recognize and honor your value as a human being, when you come to a place where you are no longer willing to compromise your own sense of dignity by tolerating abuse of any kind. This happens when loving yourself merges with accepting that you are a precious gift and dearly loved by God. There is a shift that takes place in both your mind and your heart when you begin to believe this, the results of which will change your life forever.

I now realize that, from the very beginning, God desired good things for me. He wanted me to be in a safe, nurturing, and genuinely loving relationship. God loved me then, and He loves you now. He can and will give you strength to make a change, to walk away, to pursue healing, wholeness, and true peace.

This is what I hope for you today: that you will be unafraid to tell your faith story, the real, unedited, raw, honest version. I want you to feel free to talk about the past, what you believed then, and what you believe now. I encourage you to ask tough questions of God and to know that He will help you find answers.

I know there have been many times when you have felt alone, afraid, and confused, uncertain of whom you could really trust. You may be angry with God for not caring, not helping, not rescuing you. Like me, you may have wondered, *Is God listening to me at all?* You may have cried bitter tears, thinking, *What did I do to cause him to lash out at me?* Or perhaps you have thought, *If I pray just a little bit more, believe with all my heart, do more "nice" things, forgive more, and continue to question myself less . . . perhaps then he will love me more and stop hurting me.*

Your situation can be even more confusing if you are married or in a relationship with a man who calls himself a person of faith. As I was, you may be with someone who appears to have integrity at church or in public and then is abusive behind closed doors. You may feel frustration, embarrassment, and desperation. You may feel like giving up on God because you have prayed so fervently and have not seen the results you hoped for. You might be hoping for a miracle and not seeing one.

My encouragement to you is get honest. Get honest with God and with yourself. His shoulders are big enough to carry whatever you send His way. He knows your heart anyhow. You can't pull any punches with God.

As you cry and talk to God, don't be afraid to say how you really feel. Say what you really think about God. Then sit back and wait. I believe God desires our honesty and transparency. Being truly honest with God is liberating.

After all, why fake it? Until you are gut-level honest about your true feelings, a wall will remain between you and God. The wall was not put there by Him. You laid it brick by brick in an attempt to insulate yourself from further pain. In the end, the only one walled in is you.

No matter what your faith story may be, you have the opportunity to find help, healing, and comfort by understanding some important truths about the heart and character of God.

Truth #1: God Did Not Cause Your Pain

God is not the cause of your pain. Your abuser alone is responsible for his abusive behavior. Remember, you did not cause him to abuse. Abuse is a mind-set and a choice. God is not responsible for your abuser's behavior any more than you are.

Placing responsibility where it belongs is so important to your healing. Misplacing this responsibility will only keep you stuck, whether you are blaming God or blaming yourself. Knowing that the responsibility for the abuse can be placed only at the feet of your abuser—and nowhere else—is enormously instrumental in setting you free.

If we were sitting together right now, talking about this very delicate and understandably painful subject matter, this would be precisely the moment when the nurturer in me would want to give you a gentle hug. Pain drives so many people away from God. It almost happened to me too. I was so angry with God, so hurt, and so incredibly disappointed over His apparent apathy.

But I have learned and now cling to the truth that God is good. He did not cause my pain, nor did He want me to experience the abuse. The abuse I suffered was not God's fault. He did not will it, and I did not deserve it. Did you hear that last part? *You did not deserve it!*

I believe that these thoughts of doubt and self-accusation are signs of a spiritual battle going on within you. I know because I experienced this myself. Have you ever seen those childhood cartoons in which a devil and an angel are perched on someone's shoulders giving them conflicting advice? While I don't believe there are actual figures perched on my shoulders, I do believe the mental battle within me can be a sign of a spiritual conflict. God has given each of us the gift of freedom, which means we are free to think, believe, and act any way we wish. While some of our decisions are good ones, others can bring us pain or even drive us further from God.

While God loves us and desires the very best for us, He does not force His will on us, even if it is for our own good. And if God does not force His will on us, what makes us think we can force our desires on another person? No matter how desperately we may want our abusive partners to change, we have absolutely no control over whether they will choose to do so.

So often we forget this, and we think we can control or influence the actions of our abusive partners. We also can sometimes take on the guilt that is truly theirs. But the truth is that they alone chose to do harm. Each of us has the responsibility to choose for ourselves how we will live. This means that God is not to blame for your abuser's choices, nor are you to blame for his choices.

Some women falsely equate enduring abuse with developing godliness. Perhaps they have been led to think their abusive situation is a cross they must bear. They have come to believe that if they remain faithful through the abuse, they will become more like Jesus, or they will win their husbands over without a word through their quiet and gentle spirit. This is a deadly lie.

It's true that in this world we *will* suffer. We may be laid off from work, get diagnosed with a terminal illness, or get in a car accident. These are all examples of bad things that can happen to good people. But abuse is different. Abuse is evil and there is no good in it. No one needs to stick around to be abused. Not me and not you.

Abuse is never of God. He does not want you to be anyone's whipping post. God definitely used this extremely painful time in my life for good, but He did not endorse or ignore Ben's actions. Understanding and accepting that God was never to blame for my pain kept me from going down the wrong path. Your suffering was not God's choice, and it is not His fault. It is not yours either. Understanding these foundational truths about God and yourself is paramount to healing well.

Truth #2: God Has Been with You All Along

Nevertheless, you may be wondering, *Where was God all the nights I cried myself to sleep? Where was He when I was called dirty names, pummeled like a punching bag, or treated in other deplorable ways?* The infallible truth is that God was with you all along. He cried when you cried. He hurt when you hurt. He was with you when you felt so utterly alone.

Paul, in the book of Romans, reminds us, "For I am convinced that neither death nor life, neither angels nor demons, neither the present nor the future, nor any powers, neither height nor depth, nor anything else in all creation, will be able to separate us from the love of God that is in Christ Jesus our Lord" (8:38–39). Isn't it comforting to know that no matter where we go, God sees us? There is no place we can go where His love will not reach us.

This also means that God is with us always, even in times of trouble. God is with us during our happiest times and in our most difficult moments. Even when we feel alone, we can be assured that God is with us. Our struggle to believe in Him does not push Him out of our lives.

As a mother, I love my children. It doesn't matter what they do or where they go. Even if they are far from me, I still love them and care about them. Even when they are angry at me or hide things from me, my love never fades. And God's love for us far surpasses a mother's ability to love her children.

God knows you intimately, and He cares about you. He sees you when you go through happy times, and He sees you at your worst. Psalm 56:8 says, "You keep track of all my sorrows. You have collected all my tears in your bottle. You have recorded each one in your book" (NLT). If you have never read the Psalms, you may find them especially helpful as you walk through your healing journey. Each psalm is written as a prayer, an honest, gut-wrenching conversation with God. Some of them are filled with pain, but they also declare hope and trust in God.

God is always there as a significant part of your story even when you don't feel Him. And He desires to be a significant part of your healing journey. He can be Someone to lean on, Someone to draw strength from, and ultimately the only One who can heal the broken places inside you.

Truth #3: God Wants to Set You Free

Jesus taught that God is love and, as the song says, "a good, good Father." He is the most loving and generous of fathers. He is not only aware of the abuse that is kept a secret but He's also ready and willing to provide a means of escape as He leads us to a safe place. Psalm 18 says:

> He reached down from heaven and rescued me;
>   he drew me out of deep waters.
> He rescued me from my powerful enemies,
>   from those who hated me and were too strong for me.

> They attacked me at a moment when I was in distress,
> but the LORD supported me.
> He led me to a place of safety;
> he rescued me because he delights in me.
> The LORD rewarded me for doing right;
> he restored me because of my innocence. (vv. 16–20 NLT)

I clung to this passage for dear life. It was my go-to promise in the Bible for years. I would read it and reread it when I felt I couldn't go on. This promise seemed to be the only one, for me personally, that could penetrate the pain that engulfed me. If you do not have a promise in God's Word that comforts you like this, I encourage you to search for one. It's in there. You just need to look. (Or we can share this one.)

While you may not *feel* free, you can be certain that God's deepest desire is for you to *be* free. Scripture teaches that Jesus actually came to offer you freedom; it's a gift. And the freedom He offers is not contingent on how good you are or how nice and neat your life is. Think about it. If I went out and bought a gift with you specifically in mind, would you tell me, "No thanks"? It is the same thing here but on a scale far beyond what I can describe. I hope today, as you read this page, you will stop and consider Jesus's gift. It's free for you to accept, only because He already paid for it with His life, and it has your name on it.

Our circumstances can fool us into thinking things about God that simply aren't true. God is closer than you realize. And above all, He wants you to experience freedom in every area of your life. Even if you are struggling with your belief in God, know I am praying for you. My prayer is that you will come to see yourself as God does and that you will understand His true heart for you. He desires to set you free. It is my prayer that you will soon discover you can be free to live again, no longer trudging through each day in pain. But instead, you will be free—*really* free.

Questions to Ponder

1. Take some time to write out your faith story. When you think of church and God, do you feel comforted? Or are your memories hurtful or oppressive? Maybe, like me, you began your faith journey as a child, but it took a different turn as an adult. Describe your faith story and its impact on you today.

2. How has experiencing the pain of an abusive relationship affected your relationship with God?

3. Have you ever found yourself blaming God? Are you angry? Disappointed? Confused about Him? I encourage you to express your honest thoughts and feelings toward God. Do not be afraid to speak truth. His love for you is so incredible that nothing you can say will diminish His love for you.

4. What concepts in this chapter were particularly meaningful to you? Write down one or two ideas and reflect on them this next week.

Prayer of Reflection

God, I have asked You questions, and I still struggle to find answers that bring me lasting comfort. My faith has faltered at times not knowing where You were in the midst of my pain. Often I called out to You but felt and heard nothing. Were You there? And if so, why couldn't I feel You or hear You speak to me? I want to trust You and believe You will restore my life. I also know I cannot fool You. So I choose to be honest with You today, to tell You my doubts, my fears, and even my struggle to believe.

Like the man in the Bible who asked You to heal his son in response to Your question, "Do you believe?" answered, "I believe, help me with my unbelief." This is me, Jesus. I believe, and at the same time, I am filled with unbelief. This is where I'm at: I sit in the middle of doubt, at the crossroads of belief and unbelief. You alone can help me walk the road of believing again. Down deep, I know this is true. When I struggle to believe You care, You hear me. Please wash away my doubts and fill me with faith to trust You without wavering. Thank You for allowing me to be honest with You. I bring all my questions, my fears, and my doubts to You. I lay them at the foot of Your cross. Lead me in the way I should go. Make my path clear. Help me to choose freedom for myself. Open my ears and my heart to really hear Your voice. Please quiet the clamoring within me and still my troubled soul. Lead me beside still waters, and give me peace. Amen.

God's Enduring Promises

Answer me when I call to you,
  my righteous God.
Give me relief from my distress;
  have mercy on me and hear my prayer. (Psalm 4:1)

I am worn out from my groaning.
  All night long I flood my bed with weeping
  and drench my couch with tears.
My eyes grow weak with sorrow;
  they fail because of all my foes.
Away from me, all you who do evil,
  for the LORD has heard my weeping.
The LORD has heard my cry for mercy;
  the LORD accepts my prayer. (Psalm 6:6–9)

You, LORD, hear the desire of the afflicted;
  you encourage them, and you listen to their cry.
    (Psalm 10:17)

For I am convinced that neither death nor life, neither angels nor demons, neither the present nor the future, nor any powers, neither height nor depth, nor anything else in all creation, will be able to separate us from the love of God that is in Christ Jesus our Lord. (Romans 8:38–39)

9

Do I Stay or Do I Go?

When I've asked an audience, my class, or any random individual, "What's the first question that comes to mind when you think about the subject of domestic violence?" what do you think they tell me? The most common response is, "Why doesn't she just leave?" I find it very interesting that I don't hear, "Why does he abuse her?" I find it even more disturbing that the word *just* precedes the word *leave* in their response. Believing that *just* leaving is a simple solution couldn't be further from the truth when it comes to abusive relationships! They are complicated, confusing, and anything but easy to leave.

"When my sister called that day, I told her what was happening, and she said to me, 'Just leave him,'" Kate confided. "She made it sound so simple. For a few minutes, talking with her, I believed maybe it was just that simple. That was when I decided to leave. But after I threw my things together in a bag, he was standing there in the doorway. I literally could not get past him. He wasn't a big man, but he was strong. The thing was, standing there looking at him, I didn't know what face I was about to see. He could be

113

Prince Charming one minute or Mr. Monster the next. It was that not knowing that kept me immobilized for so long."

Leaving can be fatal, and the statistics validate this. Also, as Kate's experience illustrates, what can be immensely confusing is that often the abuser presents a dual personality in the sense that he is sometimes Dr. Jekyll and sometimes Mr. Hyde. You fell in love with Dr. Jekyll. You're petrified of Mr. Hyde. When faced with the decision to stay or to go, the truth is you will be leaving both men in one body.

When I explain this to clients, they often get this look on their faces that says, "She gets it! Dr. Ramona gets that he's not always like this." I do get it. I remind them, however, that no amount of abuse is okay. Zero tolerance is the standard to uphold for themselves. That's when I pull their abuse evaluation form from their file. I hand it to them and ask them which of the abusive behaviors they circled they would be okay with someone doing to one of their kids or someone they love. I have yet to hear a single client state she would tolerate any of it.

Why We Stay

I want to be very clear: I absolutely realize how massively difficult (or seemingly impossible) it is to disentangle yourself from this relationship. I left many times myself only to turn around and go back. Most victims leave on average six to eight times before leaving for good. It will never be easy to leave. In all likelihood, you will never "feel" like you have the strength and all the resources to follow through on leaving and permanently letting go. It's understandable why the decision to leave appears to be so insurmountable. Yet what appears to be and what can be are light-years apart. What "appears to be" will continue to be your reality as long as you allow fear to hold you hostage. What "can be" takes courage. Courage is not the absence of fear. Courage is making the hard decision in the face of fear. Despite what you feel or what you believe about yourself, the truth is you are much stronger than you realize. If you're struggling to believe this, you may need to "believe in my belief" until you can believe it for yourself. That's okay. You're staying the course, and that's what matters most.

Now let's take a look at some of the most common reasons a victim remains in an abusive relationship. The reasons for staying can be the same regardless of gender (please refer to appendix F for a more complete list):

- You have financial concerns.
- You have child custody fears (you don't want the children to be alone with him).
- You are under pressure from family members to work it out.
- Due to religious beliefs, you think it's wrong to leave.
- You have a lack of social support.
- You worry no one will believe you.
- You fear he will kill you and/or the children if you attempt to leave.
- You believe he will kill himself if you leave.
- You believe he will hurt the family pet if you leave (and no domestic shelter will accept pets).
- You have nowhere to go.
- You have minimal education and/or work experience.
- You have been convinced that you are responsible for his abusive behavior (i.e., you provoke him).
- You still love him.

Does this last one surprise you? For most of you, probably not. Yet I rarely hear it mentioned in discussions of why a victim stays in an abusive relationship. Remember, abusers are some of the world's greatest manipulators. The early stages of what later becomes an abusive relationship typically start off with passion, excitement, and a sense of being swept off your feet. Combine this with a victim's super-traits and you have a recipe for disaster. To further complicate matters, Mr. Hyde doesn't show up until after Dr. Jekyll has secured his conquest. Once Jekyll senses your attachment to him, Hyde begins to emerge.

If you don't believe this, think about it. Why are you walking on eggshells during the tension-building phase as the cycle of abuse encircles you? It's because in your gut you instinctively know that Jekyll is the big cover-up for Hyde. Hyde is literally hiding around the corner. The problem is you don't know which corner.

Despite all this, your love for Jekyll is real, and real love is hard to turn off. In my opinion, it's often nearly impossible. What's important to realize is that although you may still love Jekyll, he is actually the more dangerous of the two. Why is this so? It's because he is the ultimate deceiver. He was the one who manipulated you. Jekyll cannot be trusted any more than Hyde.

What I learned through my own healing process is that to truly have a healthy love with someone, you must first have a healthy love for yourself. The years I allowed Ben to hurt and abuse me I clearly did not understand what having a healthy love for myself looked like or how to actualize it. Understanding this and pursuing it will be a crucial turning point in your own healing journey. We'll talk more about how to develop a healthy love for yourself in a later chapter.

As you remain committed to healing well, you will come to that crossroads of decision where you ask yourself, "Is this the life I want? Is this how I want to be treated? Is this healthy love?" And the ultimate question you need to answer is, "By permitting my partner to abuse me . . . am I loving myself?"

Why We Go

"I knew I was done. I was scared for my life he would make good on his threats. And if I didn't leave now, then when?" Gloria said as she stared out the window in my office. "So I told him I would run to Jack in the Box to get him some lunch. With my baby in my arms, I grabbed my purse and car keys. As I drove away, I watched our little house get smaller and smaller in the rearview mirror. I was shaking like a leaf, but I knew in my gut this was my window of opportunity to finally break free from the hell I was in. I was able to stay at a friend's place for a few days, then I boarded a plane. I have never regretted my decision. I shudder to think what our lives would have been like had I stayed."

Your situation may not be like Gloria's in which you fear for your life. Or perhaps you are faced with this same kind of terror. Be careful not to compare your situation to someone else's. This is not about comparisons. This is about choosing an abuse-free life for yourself. So regardless of where you fall on the spectrum of abuse, you still get to decide what you want your life to be like. You may find that your reason for leaving doesn't even appear on the list below. That's not what matters. What matters is that you don't allow a fear of the unknown to keep you from the life you deserve.

There are many reasons a victim chooses to leave (see appendix G). They include:

- You believe the next abusive incident could be fatal.
- He is either sexually or physically abusing the children.
- The children are acting abusive, and you realize you need to remove them from the abusive situation.
- You are informed of available help via internet, radio, TV, church, etc.
- You are encouraged by other women who have left.
- You receive the support you need from a friend, family member, counselor, or church leader.
- You are learning to truly love yourself.

Do any of the reasons listed above resonate with your particular situation? Even if not a single example does, the last one can. You can learn to truly love yourself. When it comes to needing a reason to leave, you only need this one. On the other hand, if you think about your reasons for staying in the relationship, you will notice each is fueled by fear, anxiety, faulty assumptions, or lies. As you work with your counselor or talk with a trusted friend and continue working through this book, you will learn to have a healthy love and respect for yourself. The direct result will be that you no longer tolerate abuse of any kind.

Is Change Possible?

There is only one legitimate and safe reason a person may choose to stay in a relationship that has been abusive. That is if the abusive partner *truly* has changed. I implore you to recognize I did not say "is changing" but "has changed."

Statistically, it is highly improbable that genuine and lasting change will occur. According to the Family and Child Abuse Prevention Center only "one percent of abusers change."[1] The National Domestic Violence Hotline reiterates this finding: "There's a *very* low percentage of abusers who truly do change their ways."[2] There's too much an abuser relinquishes when power and control cease (see appendix H for reasons abusers don't change). As the tagline for Emerge, the first counseling and education program to stop domestic violence in the United States, succinctly states, "Because wanting to stop is not enough."[3]

There are, however, clear indicators that sincere change has happened. These observable signs will help you discern whether your abuser is faking change or is continuing to do the genuine work necessary to make lasting change a reality. Clear signs of authentic change include the following[4] (see appendix I):

- Admits abuse toward current/past partners was unconditionally wrong
- Acknowledges his behavior was a choice, not a loss of control
- Recognizes the effects his abuse had on her and the children; shows empathy
- Identifies his pattern of controlling behaviors and entitled attitudes in detail
- Develops respectful behaviors/attitudes to replace abusive ones
- Replaces his distorted image of her with a positive, empathetic view
- Accepts the consequences of his abusive actions and commits to not repeat them
- Makes amends
- Accepts overcoming abusiveness is likely a lifelong process
- Remains accountable for past and future actions

The above verifiable indicators of change are not pick-and-choose options for an abuser. He must do them all. No exceptions.

Lundy Bancroft was part of the Emerge team that launched the very first abusive men's group in 1977. He has worked with thousands of abusive men. His research indicates that an abuser who holds onto his core entitlements will ultimately abuse again. By protecting even one privilege, he will revert back to some or all of his abusive, controlling behaviors. Bancroft's counsel is solid, and I would strongly encourage you to heed it.

Equally important is knowing if your abusive partner is not exhibiting legitimate change. Below are Bancroft's indicators that an abuser has not changed[5] (see appendix J):

- Says he can change only if she changes and "helps" him change
- Criticizes her for not realizing how much he's changed

- Criticizes her for considering him capable of behaving abusively even though he's done so in the past
- Reminds her of the bad things he would have done, but doesn't anymore, amounting to a subtle threat
- Tells her she's taking too long to make up her mind, pressuring her not to take the time she needs to assess his change
- Says he's changing, but she doesn't feel it

My Crossroads Decision

I can remember vividly the moment I came to my crossroads decision. I was sitting on the bedroom floor, looking out at the moon through the window, talking on the phone with a precious friend and respected mentor. He'd been Ben's and my professor in undergraduate school and had counseled us in the very early years of our marriage. He was dearly loved by the students and highly respected by the faculty. It was clear to all who knew him that he truly loved Jesus and loved people. His character and genuine compassion for people were reflected in both his behavior and his choices.

I was deeply deliberating over whether to leave the marriage or to keep trying. At the risk of sounding grandiose, if there was an Olympic event in marital loyalty, perseverance, and believing the best (despite the evidence), I was a gold medalist! Many of you also took a gold medal in this same event! I was Queen Super-traits and thought at the time that this was a noble thing. Boy, have I come a long way since then.

That night I'd called my mentor for counsel, and, ever the good student, I sat poised, notebook and pencil in hand, as I listened to my mentor share with me from his heart. I took eleven pages of notes that night! I am not even kidding! Now remember, I had left many times in the past but had always returned with the erroneous belief that Ben would change this time.

As I listened intently, my mentor came to a point in the conversation where he asked me a very powerful question. Knowing the abuse I had endured over the years in my marriage, he asked, "Do you believe that when you get to heaven Jesus is going to put a gold star on your forehead for a good job? You did it! You stayed!" Honestly, I was taken aback by his question. I was expecting him, and I'm not sure exactly why, to say "Just pray more, believe more that God can do a miracle." Instead, he gently reminded me of this truth: God does do miracles, but He does not override our will. My miracle was the resolve and the energy God was going to give me to leave and leave for good.

God was not going to change Ben unless Ben desired to be changed. You see, free will is a gift God gives each of us. How we choose to use that gift is up to us. I could see that Ben's behavior over and over again clearly demonstrated he had no intention of changing. We must also realize that God does not give out gold stars to those who hang in there, enduring suffering without reason. I was suffering. So were my children from seeing the abuse. I was experiencing night terrors on a regular basis. Night terrors are akin to nightmares, but on steroids. Many nights I jumped out of bed in utter horror thinking I was going to be killed. One night I even ran into the wall and knocked myself unconscious. I woke up with my head cupped in my hands in a puddle of my own blood. My body was sending me undeniable warning signs that I desperately needed to leave. To let go. To move on. I finally listened. I chose to go and with this choice hired an attorney to represent me in my divorce.

As I have repeatedly stated, these situations are anything but simple. Over the next three years, I went through three attorneys. My first attorney was intimidated by Ben. I requested that she pursue a court-mandated batterer's intervention program for him. Rather than poke the giant, she looked straight into my eyes and curtly responded, "Ramona, nobody cares!" My second lawyer treated me unethically. I'm not going to expound on that one. Suffice it to say, his conduct is the reason attorneys sometimes get a bad rap. However, my last attorney was a gentleman in every sense of the word. Plus, he was not afraid of Ben and saw him for the true coward he was, stating with conviction, "Real men don't hit their wives." I hold deep respect for this man and will always be grateful to him. I asked him point-blank, "Will you protect us? The kids and I are counting on you." He said yes and kept his promise.

During our three-year legal separation, Ben and I went to individual counseling and joined our own respective support groups. He attended a men's group, and I attended a women's group. We also went to a weeklong, one-on-one program with a psychologist to "save the marriage." And here comes the punch line . . . I took him back. You heard me right. Once again I leaned on my super-traits of loyalty, empathy, and tolerance while ignoring my gut and hoped for a miracle. I imagine by now you may be thinking, *If this woman can finally heal well, surely I can.* Well, you're right! You can and you are. I promised you I was going to be completely transparent.

During the four months that I took him back, he dropped out of counseling and within weeks began to abuse me again. Remember, abusers very seldom change. Mine clearly didn't. At last, I was ready to stop ignoring my gut and believe the truth. It then took another three years, after I hired my third attorney, to complete the divorce.

Abuse Severs the Marriage Covenant

I was raised in a home where I was taught that divorce was never an option, but I have come to understand that it can be a very viable and healthy decision for victims of domestic violence.

Let me explain what I mean. Jesus came to set us free (Galatians 5:1). When the institution of marriage is placed above the individual, there's a problem. Jesus died for people, not for institutions.

As a matter of fact, the Bible tells us that there is no marriage or giving in marriage in heaven. This does not diminish the importance of marriage on earth, but it does demonstrate that we should not place more value on the institution than on the person.

In my practice, I've heard some victims of domestic violence confess that they think divorce is an option only if there has been sexual infidelity. Please hear me: that is ludicrous. God is a loving God. He would *never* advocate tolerating abuse in order to maintain a marriage. Violence within a marriage breaks the marital covenant. Period. If a victim chooses to divorce, she is simply carrying out legally what her abusive partner already broke spiritually. Abuse has already severed the sacred covenant. In fact, the official position of the United States Conference of Catholic Bishops regarding domestic violence and divorce is this: "Violence and abuse, not divorce, break up a marriage."[6] (If you would like additional information regarding what the Bible teaches about divorce and domestic violence, refer to appendix K.)

So, like me, you find yourself at a crossroads. Your abuser has not changed. Leaving is an option you're strongly considering. You've accepted that the only way to end the cycle of abuse is to no longer be a part of it. While making the decision to leave an abusive relationship is complicated and difficult on many levels, it ultimately can save your life and the lives of your children. Regardless of where your relationship may be on the abuse continuum, abuse always escalates. Even if you do not believe your life is currently in physical danger, living with abuse of any kind is slowly destroying you on the inside. This is a fact. Do you love yourself enough to leave? Good! Then it's a momentous moment. A hopeful moment. It's time to make preparations.

(Note: If you're not quite there yet, please reread previous sections of this book and take more time to process them. When you're ready, continue working through the book. I'm praying for you—for strength, courage, and an openness to love yourself in ways you never deemed possible. I have an actual prayer team of wonderful women who have committed to praying for my readers. You are not alone.)

Maneuvers Your Abuser May Use to Keep You from Leaving

Contrary to what many people think, leaving a nonabusive partner is generally much easier than leaving an abusive one. Few abusers readily allow themselves to be left without challenging the decision. As your abuser senses you getting stronger—setting healthy and consistent boundaries and learning to love yourself—he will interpret all of this as a threat to his power and ability to control you. I want to make you keenly aware of the maneuvers your abuser may use in an attempt to keep you from leaving.[7]

- Promises to change
- Enters therapy or an abusers' program
- Stops drinking/attends AA
- Apologizes
- Says no one else will want you
- Says you're abandoning him
- Threatens to kidnap/take custody of the children
- Threatens to withhold finances
- Acts nice
- Persuades others to pressure you into giving him another chance
- Threatens suicide
- Spreads rumors or your confidential information
- Starts a relationship/affair to upset you
- Insists he's changed
- Threatens or assaults anyone helping you or starting a relationship with you

- Gets you pregnant
- Stalks you
- Physically/sexually assaults you
- Destroys property
- Threatens to harm or kill you

When you observe any of these things happening, remind yourself that they are tactics to manipulate you and are not indicators of true change. (This list of maneuvers an abuser may use to keep you from leaving can also be found on Appendix L.)

Crucial Next Steps: Safety Planning

Your most important preparation is safety planning. Statistically speaking, when a victim of domestic violence leaves, she is at the greatest risk for injury or even fatality. This is precisely why it is crucial (when possible) to have the support, guidance, and counsel of a trained therapist to assist you in structuring your plan. A safety plan needs to fit your unique needs and situation. The best safety plans are personalized and practical. I have included three plans in appendix B to provide you with helpful information regardless of where you may be in the leaving process. The safety plans cover preparing to leave, when you are leaving, and after you have left.

It's imperative that you discuss your plan thoroughly with your counselor and/or trusted family members and friends. Letting others know about your situation increases your level of safety. Provide your children's school, a trusted neighbor (if possible), and a friend with a copy of your restraining order, if you have obtained one.

The value of a well-thought-out safety plan cannot be overemphasized. When we are in a crisis situation, our ability to think clearly is impaired. By preparing in advance what items you will need and practicing how you will respond in various scenarios, you will increase the likelihood of a safe departure. I also strongly suggest contacting the National Domestic Violence Hotline ahead of time to discuss resources available in your area. You can reach them at www.TheHotline.org. (Please refer to appendix C for additional hotlines and resources.)

In appendix M, I have also included the danger signs indicating an abuser may turn violent when you attempt to leave. It is vital you are familiar with this information before you attempt to leave. I also strongly encourage you to discuss this material with your counselor or a trusted confidant. Notify the police immediately if you even remotely sense your safety is in jeopardy. You are learning to turn up the volume on your gut. When preparing to leave and thereafter, it is paramount that you trust the gift of your gut.

Your Best Years Are Ahead of You

I want to say how very proud I am of you and how excited I am for you. You have come a long way regardless of where you are in your particular journey. It takes tremendous courage and strength to do what you've done. What matters most is that you've chosen a different path for yourself. You've chosen not to allow the trauma of abuse to dictate your future or how you view yourself.

Healing well and living free are not reserved for a select few. They are choices each of us can make. They involve a day-by-day commitment to keep growing, keep believing, and keep holding on to faith that the best years of our lives are ahead of us.

One of my absolute favorite verses is Psalm 84:6. It says that when we walk through the valley of weeping, it will become a place of refreshing springs and autumn rains. It's a short little verse, but it is packed with a ton of wisdom and comfort. Notice the pace is a *walk*, not a run. That's why this healing well quest you're on seems like it is taking so long. Next, notice we are meant to go *through* and not set up camp in the valley of weeping. And finally, the incredible promise is that the places that caused weeping in our lives *will become* (this indicates it's a process and not a quick fix) a place of refreshing springs and autumn rains. In other words, the very areas of pain in our lives will become places of blessing and victory. This is an awesome promise!

Clearly, you've been walking through your own personal "valley of weeping" for a long time. Be encouraged, you are walking through. As you continue healing well, the places of deepest anguish in your life will become the very areas you experience the greatest blessings. Only with God is this possible. You and Jesus together are walking through your valley. Others will come alongside you for a portion, but only Jesus will be with you until you are out the other side. Keep holding His hand. Keep walking!

Questions to Ponder

1. Below is a list of reasons someone may choose to remain in an abusive relationship. Mark any of the reasons you have stayed or add your own to the list.

   □ You fear your abuser will become more violent, perhaps fatally so, if you try to leave.

   □ You want to protect your partner's and your family's image.

   □ Your partner is your support system, even though he is abusive. Psychologically, he has destroyed your outside relationships.

   □ You think this time will be the last time; he will change.

   □ You fear being a single parent with a reduced income.

   □ You fear he will stalk you and harass you at your workplace.

   □ You do not realize you have the right *not* to be abused.

   □ Your only desire for change is *not to be abused.*

   □ You fear living alone.

☐ You were raised in an abusive home, and this feels normal.

☐ You think the abuse will stop if you will only . . .

☐ Religious and cultural beliefs keep you in the marriage.

☐ You stay for the children; any father is better than none.

☐ Your confidence has deteriorated as a result of continuous put-downs, name-calling, or other forms of abusive behavior.

☐ You have no place to go. Often friends and family are not helpful.

☐ You have feelings of powerlessness and fear.

☐ You believe that all you have in life is your family, house, children, husband, and/or marriage. They are your responsibility, and you must fix whatever goes wrong.

☐ You believe divorce is not a viable option.

☐ He is not always abusive. After the violence, he is often contrite, asking for forgiveness, promising change, and acting like the model father and husband . . . for a while.

☐ You feel trapped and do not know about help services.

☐ You believe that if you disclose the secret, no one will believe you. He is a pillar in the community and/or church.

☐ You believe the law will not take you seriously and that he will not be punished.

☐ You fear the complexities of the legal system. Lawyers are expensive.

☐ You still love him.

☐ _____

_____

_____

☐ _____

_____

_____

Have you ever left for a while only to return and watch the cycle repeat itself? Please refrain from shaming yourself for this choice. Leaving is a difficult decision. Take the time you need to make the best decision for yourself.

2. If you have left the abusive relationship, why did you choose to leave? Take a moment to write out the reasons you left and reread them as you continue working through this book. Check off any of the reasons below that apply to your story. Remind yourself daily that choosing an abuse-free life was one of the greatest gifts you could ever give yourself. Remember, only you can choose you.

☐ You believed the next abusive incident could be fatal.

☐ He was either sexually or physically abusing the children.

☐ The children were acting abusive, and you realized you needed to remove them from the abusive situation.

☐ You were informed of available help via internet, radio, TV, church, etc.

☐ You were encouraged by other women who had left.

☐ You received the support you needed from a friend, family member, counselor, or church.

☐ You were learning to truly love yourself.

☐ _____

_____

☐ _____

_____

3. Describe how you are learning to love yourself in a healthier way. List some observable indicators that this positive change is happening.

4. Can you identify any mental roadblocks to having a healthy love for yourself? If so, do you realize these are faulty beliefs?

For every faulty belief you have regarding yourself, write it down along with a statement of truth to replace it.
Examples:

Faulty belief: I made the decision to get into this relationship. Now I must make the best of it.

Truth: No one should ever live with abuse. It's imperative that I learn to have a healthy love for myself. Healthy love does not tolerate abuse.

Faulty belief: I am not able to support myself. I need him to take care of me.

Truth: I have gifts and talents that are uniquely mine. I am capable of meeting my needs. If necessary, I can get training or education to support myself (and my children). I am strong.

5. What are your thoughts regarding divorce? How has the information in this chapter affected what you believe about this subject? Do you recognize now that remaining in an abusive situation is not God's desire for you or your cross to bear?

Prayer of Reflection

Jesus, I'm at a crossroads. I've been sitting at this intersection in my life for way too long. It's time to make a decision. I'm comforted in knowing that You've sat next to me this entire time and that You have no intention of ever leaving me. My reasons for staying seemed to make sense to me at the time. But I'm learning that it's not important why I stayed but why I leave. Leaving is loving myself. Leaving the abuse is loving my children. I need Your help. I can't do this without You.

I'm still confused at times. Clear my thoughts. Lead my steps. Teach me what it means to love myself as You love me. I'm scared. Please comfort me as only You can. Wrap Your arms of protection around me and my children. Hold us tightly to Your chest. Allow me to feel Your embrace if I'm ever tempted to turn back or doubt my decision. Thank You for continuing to hold my hand as together we walk through this dark valley of weeping. Knowing this valley will become a place of blessing is the encouragement and reminder I need to keep walking. Lead me out to the other side. There is life, a great life, after abuse. Show me the way. Amen.

God's Enduring Promises

When they walk through the Valley of Weeping,
    it will become a place of refreshing springs.
    The autumn rains will clothe it with blessings. (Psalm
       84:6 NLT)

He will redeem them from oppression and violence,
    for their lives are precious to him. (Psalm 72:14 NLT)

O Lord, rescue me from evil people.
    Protect me from those who are violent. (Psalm 140:1 NLT)

"All your children shall be taught by the Lord,
And great shall be the peace of your children.
In righteousness you shall be established;
You shall be far from oppression, for you shall not fear;
And from terror, for it shall not come near you. . . .
No weapon formed against you shall prosper,
And every tongue which rises against you in judgment
You shall condemn.

This is the heritage of the servants of the LORD,
And their righteousness is from Me,"
Says the LORD. (Isaiah 54:13–14, 17 NKJV)

(Note: While in an abusive relationship, you certainly are not in a safe place. God's desire is that you live in peace and safety. Continue to trust and walk with Him as He leads you out.)

The work of righteousness will be peace,
And the effect of righteousness, quietness and assurance
forever.
My people will dwell in a peaceful habitation,
In secure dwellings, and in quiet resting places. (Isaiah
32:17–18 NKJV)

I will both lie down in peace, and sleep;
For You alone, O LORD, make me dwell in safety. (Psalm
4:8 NKJV)

10

I'm Out, but I Still Feel Stuck

When my children were young, they loved to ride the tea cups at Disneyland, or any ride that spun us around like clothes in a rinse cycle. When the ride ended, they would scramble to get back in line, never skipping a beat. I, on the other hand, felt my head spinning for hours and my stomach still protesting.

Surviving an abusive relationship can leave you feeling like you are "spinning" long after you exit. Understandably, feeling and thinking clearly can be tough in the wake of so much emotional upheaval. Healing well takes time. For most, it takes a long time. Exiting the crazy ride is good, but the stress does not stop simply because you are no longer living with an abuser. Understanding this can help you avoid confusion and a myriad of other emotions.

One of the things I did to help keep perspective during this time in my healing journey was to reflect on my journal entries as well as the notes I sometimes took during counseling. History doesn't lie. Your history is your story, and your story is your truth. One of the best ways that I found to continue plodding forward was to take a brief glance back into my past. Reviewing my counseling notes or my journal entries was the splash in the face I needed to reaffirm that I was moving in the right direction and that I was gaining ground. You need to review it so you don't repeat it!

Resist the Tendency to Sugarcoat

Our human tendency is to not remember pain, so when we think back, things don't seem so bad. I believe this is a mercy God gives us. Just think if you could actually feel the pain of a broken bone or giving birth every time it crossed your mind? That would be awful! It is a gift that we cannot feel physical pain afterward; all we have is the memory of that incidence of pain, and we tend to forget how painful it was.

Such is the case with emotional pain too. With emotional pain, the danger is that we can lie to ourselves in an attempt to rewrite our past, minimizing our pain and denying the truth of how bad it really was. For example, I have witnessed this phenomenon at funerals. Family members and friends are all gathered around sharing stories, and all of a sudden, the jerk becomes a stellar citizen and a model relative. Why do people do this? Denying truth can be a temporary solution to a reality that seems easier to avoid.

It was just before Christmas, and Emma sat in my office with tears running down her cheeks. "How can I not hang Steve's stocking from the mantel? This would have been our tenth Christmas together. The kids keep asking me, 'Where is Daddy?' Maybe getting a restraining order wasn't a good idea. He wasn't always abusive. Especially during the holidays. He could be really nice."

I gently reminded Emma that she had gotten the restraining order because Steve had choked her and had a history of similar physical and verbal assaults against her. Her momentary glamorizing of the past with Steve quickly turned to, "You're right, Dr. Ramona. He hurt me in so many ways. Help me to remember this and not gloss over reality."

If you want to pass through the times you feel stuck, be aware of this tendency to sugarcoat or romanticize the past. Especially as you become stronger and walk away, your abusive partner may attempt to sweet-talk you back into the relationship, saying it wasn't so bad. It really was as bad as it was! Holding on to the truth is crucial. Only you know the whole story. So when you feel as if you aren't making progress or are tempted to gloss over or romanticize the past, take a quick glance back and then give yourself the giant hug you deserve for getting off the crazy ride.

Avoid Dating Prematurely

Equally detrimental to the healing process is if you think you are further along in the process than you really are. Believing this assumption can actually set you back. Don't give in to the pull to quit on yourself, stop counseling and/or stop reading this book. Don't do it! Just because you are feeling stronger and gaining knowledge doesn't mean you have finished the journey. And it's especially important not to short-circuit the healing process by starting another relationship prematurely. Have you ever bit into a half-baked casserole? Not good. You're on your way, but you need more time to heal. Getting into a relationship now is not a good idea. We attract where we're at. Wait until your heart and your head are in an emotionally healthy place. I will cover this topic more in a later chapter, but for now keep reading, and, I recommend staying off the dating sites!

"I joined an online dating site because I was feeling lonely. Right away I started getting emails from interested men. It was so good to feel I was attractive again," Carol confessed. "It was kind of like a drug. I started obsessively checking my phone to see if anyone might have messaged me. Pretty soon I recognized that I was looking for self-worth in the wrong place. I clearly wasn't ready to date. I deleted the dating app and focused instead on healing."

Move Forward

I firmly believe you must take a *quick* glance back to stay focused. Looking back can remind you how far you've come. But it is equally important to fix your gaze on some point up ahead so that you stay determined and make progress. I hope you have sought out a professional who is providing you with wise counsel. Stay encouraged as you continue moving forward through the healing well steps while permitting yourself the time you need to digest this information.

Make an intentional decision to focus on your future. Please notice the word *your* here. Keep in mind that your super-traits can influence where you direct your focus. Time spent in an abusive relationship can be all consuming, demanding continuous focus. Being in a relationship with an abuser is exhausting, and victims often discover that they have lost sight of who they are and what they desire to pursue in life. Now is the time to change all that. Now is the time to decide to refocus on the things that matter to you.

It may have been so long since you've done this that you don't know where to start. This shift in focus doesn't have to be huge. If you feel too uncomfortable with the shift in focus, you may avoid it altogether, and that's not going to help. Instead, refocus in incremental baby steps. Perhaps you can take a class at the local junior college that looks interesting. Or consider pursuing a hobby that you find relaxing or stimulating. I took up kickboxing for a few years. At the time, I had no clue how beneficial that decision would be. Through kickboxing, I regained a lot of my confidence, while at the same time I was able to release a ton of emotional pain that was still buried inside.

All change, whether positive or negative, begins with a decision. If you didn't want to change, you never would have picked up this book. Good decisions lead to good outcomes even when there are obstacles along the way.

In a recent conversation with one of my adult daughters, she happily shared with me what a wonderful life her best friend enjoys. When I asked my daughter why she believes her friend's life is so wonderful, she simply said, "Because she has made a lot of great decisions." Deciding to heal well is both an initial decision, when you reach that point of saying, "Enough!" and also a daily commitment you make to yourself.

I can safely assume there have been moments along the way when you have contemplated giving up and going back. And if you have not been tempted to go back, you have possibly toyed with the idea of dating prematurely or short-circuiting your healing process in some other way. If good decisions ultimately lead to good outcomes, then poor decisions work exactly the same way. It will never be a good decision to quit on yourself. What kind of life do you really want? If the answer is a good one, then stay the course. Continue to make the good decision to focus on your future and the life you deserve. You, like the rest of us, will have challenges. But let them be challenges that are not self-induced. Learn from the example of my daughter's best friend. Choose wisely. Make good decisions, and then enjoy the benefits that will eventually result from them.

Questions to Ponder

1. As you reflect on your own experience, can you see how you may have attempted to rewrite your past in order to minimize your pain and deny the truth of how bad it really was?

2. What have been some of the consequences of glamorizing the past? Have you gone back into the abusive relationship, or have you been tempted to return? Reread "Clear Signs an Abuser Has Not Changed" (appendix J) and "Maneuvers an Abuser Uses to Keep You from Leaving" (appendix L).

3. Do you struggle with feeling you aren't healing fast enough? Review your answers to the questions in previous chapters. Note areas you are making progress. What do you understand now that you didn't prior to reading this book?

4. Perhaps you believe you are further along than you actually are. If you were to ask your best friend or someone you trust, would they encourage you to stay the course as you continue healing well? We all have blind spots and cannot see things within ourselves that others sometimes can. Allow someone who truly has your best interest in mind to help you see clearly the areas within yourself that may be out of focus.

5. What good decisions have you made that you are now beginning to see the results from? What good decisions do you still need to make to experience the life you deserve?

Prayer of Reflection

I am thankful, Jesus, for all that I'm learning and for how far You have brought me. Still now, however, I feel scrambled at times. Was it that bad? I no sooner think that thought than flashbacks start to flood my mind, quickly confirming my pain is real and the abuse did happen. Help me to stop rewriting parts of my story to make it more palatable. Help me to stay firmly grounded in truth. There were some good times, but a safe relationship doesn't just have times that are good. Rather, a truly good relationship is safe all the time. Not because it is perfect but because there is no abuse. No fear. I don't want to live with fear anymore. I want to live in peace and safety. Pace my steps and enable me to receive wise counsel. If I start to run ahead of where You have me for now, please draw me back. When I struggle with doubt, gently remind me that the plans You have for me are for good, not for harm, to give me a future and a hope. Amen.

God's Enduring Promises

For I know the thoughts that I think toward you, says the LORD, thoughts of peace and not of evil, to give you a future and a hope. (Jeremiah 29:11 NKJV)

And now, dear brothers and sisters, one final thing. Fix your thoughts on what is true, and honorable, and right, and pure, and lovely, and admirable. Think about things that are excellent and worthy of praise. (Philippians 4:8 NLT)

> Trust in the LORD with all your heart,
> And lean not on your own understanding;
> In all your ways acknowledge Him,
> And He shall direct your paths. (Proverbs 3:5–6 NKJV)

Don't be impatient for the Lord to act! Keep traveling steadily along his pathway and in due season he will honor you with every blessing. (Psalm 37:34 TLB)

11

Forgiveness Frees . . . You!

Forgiveness is not a cure-all that will all of a sudden make your life happy. However, forgiveness is a huge part of the healing process. My story definitely involves a precise moment when I chose to forgive my abuser as well as a time when I decided to forgive myself. Although neither of those decisions came easily.

To help you understand what led to my decision to forgive Ben, let me share how our story ended. As you may recall, in the very beginning, I thought I was living a storybook romance fully equipped with a handsome prince (minus the horse-drawn carriage). But our marriage, like most relationships characterized by abuse, had moments of passion quickly followed by emotional, and often physical, wreckage.

The Final Betrayal

After almost two decades of holding out for a miracle, the reality that the marriage was over came to a crescendo. The self-inflicted shame I felt for staying as long as I did, coupled with my reaction to his final act of betrayal, necessitated an urgent need for a decision on my part.

Would I forgive? Could I forgive? Do I deserve to be forgiven for allowing my children to grow up in this abuse and chaos?

Since my family of origin never allowed me to consider the option of divorce for any reason other than infidelity, I held on to our marriage for many years. I hoped that my miracle was just around the bend of yet another broken promise. I finally insisted that Ben had to get help for his anger. Ben, in retaliation, filed for divorce.

(Note: Please keep in mind that at that time I didn't know what I know now. As I explained earlier, the issue was not Ben's anger; as with anyone who chooses to abuse, the issue was his choice to abuse. We all get angry, but we don't all abuse.)

At the time, Ben was working abroad, but he would soon return to the States for a two-week break. Because of his prior threats to physically hurt me, such as when he said he could snap my neck and no one would know it, I was petrified. The kids and I were living in a very rural area. There was no cell phone reception, and our house was set back two miles from the nearest country road.

So as I said, when Ben realized I really meant business, he hired an attorney, filed for divorce, and quickly emptied our bank accounts. I was served divorce papers right after Christmas and ended up returning some of our children's gifts to try to keep us financially afloat. It was horrible.

As I was being served with papers, I stood at the front door in shock. I asked the server to read me what the paperwork said. He explained that he was not supposed to do that, but I think he felt sorry for me, so he reluctantly agreed. After reading just a brief excerpt, he said, "Ma'am, my sister was married to a guy like this. I suggest you hire yourself a good attorney and protect yourself. These kinds of guys are dangerous."

Shortly after this, I did hire an attorney. Seeing that I was serious, Ben quit his job and moved back to the States. He said he wanted to be closer to me and the kids. Looking back, I see that quitting his job was more about punishing me for setting a boundary and insisting on real change than reflective of a sincere desire to be closer to us. Money, whether it was overspending or in this case underproviding, was an easy way to maintain power and control.

The divorce process stalled for a number of reasons. My super-traits were something I had leaned on all my life. So I found myself wanting to make sure I had turned over every rock doing everything I possibly could to save the marriage. At the same time, my parents were pressuring me with increasing intensity to make the marriage work. I continued seeking legal counsel while simultaneously throwing a final Hail Mary pass. I felt pulled between two opposing forces: my gut said, "I need to divorce," and my familial value system said, "Stay married no matter what."

During this time, Ben and I were legally separated and living apart. At my insistence, we both attended support groups through Life Skills International. Ben participated in a twenty-eight-week men's group, and I was involved at the same time in a group for women. My dad implored us to also attend a one-week intensive Life Skills workshop in Colorado that he would pay for. I very reluctantly agreed to his request. During that week, Ben and I met daily one-on-one with a psychologist. We were each instructed to watch videos on marriage, and we then met with the psychologist as a couple.

Since Life Skills International was founded by Dr. Paul Hegstrom, author of *Angry Men and the Women Who Love Them*, I found myself holding out hope. After all, Paul and Judy's story involved horrific domestic violence. And yet what I've come to realize is that when Judy set tough, healthy boundaries, Paul humbled himself and did the necessary work to truly change from the inside out. They ended up remarrying each other after being divorced for eight years. So I thought certainly attending these groups and the intensive one-week intervention in Colorado would yield the same outcome for us. Right? Unfortunately, I was wrong. From the room I was sitting in while taking notes on each video, I could see Ben across the hallway, lying on his back on the floor, throwing a wadded-up paper ball into the air. I could tell he was obviously not invested in the process.

As I look back, I can see that as good of a program as Life Skills is and as hard as I tried, I couldn't do it alone. I felt as if I was in a two-person rowboat, and I was the only one with an oar in the water. We were repeatedly going in circles. It's difficult to put into words just how hard I tried to save my marriage and do everything I could.

If you are or have been in a similar situation, attempting to turn over every rock trying to make the marriage work, I understand the despondency and complete exhaustion this causes. I by no means judge you. I get you, because I once was you. In my own story, my numerous attempts to bring about change did not end here. Rather, my efforts continued.

As I worked on my doctorate and sold real estate, I was able to save enough money to put a down payment on my own home. I still remember that New Year's Eve. I was sitting alone in my empty house eating Chinese food and surrounded by unpacked boxes stacked to the ceiling. My son was in Europe trying out for professional soccer. My oldest daughter and I had had a disagreement, and Ben had taken advantage of the situation to get her to temporarily move back in with him. My youngest teenage daughter, in an effort to avoid the pain going on at home, had gone out that evening with friends to an amusement park. Internally, I felt disjointed and empty. I missed my family. I missed being a mom and a wife. I was lonely.

The following morning Ben called and asked me to go for a walk. This was one of my favorite things to do, and in the past, he never wanted to do it with me. In my emotional state, I took that as a sign that perhaps we really could start over. I said yes that day. I wanted all of us to be under one roof. Two weeks later, Ben moved into my house. Our family was complete again. I was happy.

But in the most important ways, I soon realized that very little had changed. We went back into couple's counseling as well as financial counseling. While sitting with our financial counselors, Ben was questioned about a large sum of money he had spent prior to reconciling that he refused to account for. Angered by their inquiries, Ben left the meeting in a rage. I sat at the table feeling terribly embarrassed by Ben's behavior while the counselors looked at me as if to say, "Now what?"

Shortly afterward, Ben did the same thing during a meeting with our marriage counselor. The moment the counselor encouraged Ben to be accountable, he bolted for the door, leaving me sitting with yet another therapist. As I sat crying, the therapist said to me, "I don't think he has what it takes to make this work." The therapist was right.

I was at the end of my rope. In April, Ben accepted another overseas contract and left to pursue this job. In May, I started sensing that something was strange. In an email to Ben, I told him I sensed some weird juju. Later, I would discover that the juju was more than a feeling. Money continued to be an issue between us, and I noticed that funds were mysteriously missing from our accounts. Ben shrugged it off with excuses. He told me he had met a woman whose family was poor and was helping them pay bills.

In October, he returned to the States for a brief time of training and would immediately be heading back overseas. But this time things felt different. He acted more distant, and I became increasingly suspicious.

One evening my parents were coming over for dinner. That afternoon Ben went to the gym and accidentally left behind his backpack. Although I was never one to snoop, I had an overwhelming inner nudge to look inside. What I found chilled me. His phone contained text after text between him and another woman declaring their love for each other. I also found his Bible, and tucked in the pages were two pictures. One photo was of Ben and me, and the other was of the two of them. Buried at the bottom of his backpack were several letters she had written to him. In them, she expressed her concern that he had a good wife and should go back and love her. I was devastated. Even after taking him back following a three-year separation, tons of counseling, and a one-week intensive, Ben still betrayed me. I finally accepted he would never change.

I phoned my mom. I was sweating, shaking, upset. She told me, "Copy everything and put it back as you found it." That evening after dinner with my parents, my mom didn't hug Ben good-bye. As they drove away, Ben said, "What's up with her?"

I replied, "I don't know. You tell me." He then headed upstairs and went to bed. I remember looking at him sprawled across our bed sleeping and thinking, *I'm never going to lie with that guy again!* As I sat on the floor in the walk-in closet sobbing, my thoughts were racing. Not wanting to wake him, I went downstairs to calm myself and decide my next move.

As I was walking down the stairs, my seventeen-year-old son came out of his bedroom and asked, "Mama, are you okay?"

"Yes, I'm fine," I said.

But my son turned on the lights and looked at me. "You don't look fine," he said, tenderly adding, "I'm old enough now. Don't worry, you can tell me."

So we headed downstairs and sat on the couch, where I told him what I had discovered. He wept bitterly. We both sat there numb and confused, feeling a sense of betrayal that's impossible to describe. My son kept repeating, "How could Dad do this, Mom? How could he do this to us?" I had no answer for him.

In his desperation, my son wanted me to throw Ben out immediately. Due to my track record of always taking Ben back, I can understand why my son wanted me to act right then while my emotions were peaked. Not knowing how to convince my son that this time really was different, I assured him the best I could that I was going to deal with this. Things were not going to go back to status quo this time, and this time I meant it.

Right about then, Ben came downstairs to get a midnight snack, and I gave my son "the look," meaning, "Don't say a word." I then turned and headed up the stairs. As I paused on the landing, I heard my son say. "You're cheating on Mom! Why would you do that?"

Ben denied it, saying, "Your mom is crazy. She's lying!" When I heard this, I rushed back into the kitchen and pulled the copies of the letters out of my bathrobe pocket. I started reading them out loud.

Ben turned to me in a rage and tried to grab the letters out of my hand. He chased me up the stairs, but in that second, something inside me changed. I spun around and said, "I have run from you for the last time." And with that, I hauled off and slapped him with every ounce of strength I had. It felt like I hit a brick wall. Ben is a big man, and he let out a mocking laugh. "That's all you got?" he sneered as he turned and walked away.

This scene is but one of the many reasons I struggled with shame and unforgiveness toward myself for so many years. No doubt about it, Ben's actions were unconscionable. Yet at the same time, there were so many things I held against myself. Leaving Ben was the right and best thing to do. Hitting him that night was not. Knowing that my precious son watched this take place is still a deep ache I carry. Eventually, in my story, I forgave Ben. Yet forgiving myself seemed unwarranted and undeserved for so many years.

An Act of My Will

The next day Ben left for training and then headed back overseas. I was extremely depressed and felt flooded with anger. I could hardly function. I knew if I left my emotions unchecked, the growing bitterness would eventually eat away at my soul.

I know this may sound ridiculous to you, but I knew if I waited to forgive him, the pain of all the years prior, coupled with the news of his affair, would solidify the bitterness in my heart forever. I knew if I did not decide to act right then, based on my will and not my emotions, I never would.

So one night, with my youngest daughter cuddled next to me in the bed, we held hands, and I prayed. I can remember it as if it were yesterday. I said:

Jesus, the pain of all these years is beyond what my heart can bear. Now the pain of knowing he has cheated on me feels like a blow so crushing I may never recover. I need Your help. Help me to forgive. Help me to surrender this pain to You—tonight. I don't want to carry this around another day. By an act of my will, I choose to forgive. Please, Lord, help me not to pick this back up again. Make me strong, but keep me tender. I have a son, a father, and two brothers I love. I don't want to be a bitter woman who hates men. I want to love again. Set me free. Set my children free. Heal the broken places in us that only You can see. I need You. I love You. Amen.

That night was the beginning of my journey of forgiveness and, I believe, a continuation on my path toward healing well.

You see, forgiveness is not a straight route. It is messy. It is not the shortest distance between two points. As I mentioned before, it was one thing for me to extend forgiveness to Ben for all that had happened, but it was another to forgive myself. That would be by far the toughest, most heart-wrenching part of my journey.

From the onset of our relationship, I had ignored my gut. I had repeatedly attempted to set loosey-goosey boundaries, hoping they would somehow bring about the change I so desperately desired. I had seen countless tears fall down my children's cheeks. I had made so many empty promises to them that things would change, life would get better, and they would be safe. These are but a handful of the reasons why forgiving myself seemed like nothing more than a selfish act and a privilege I didn't deserve.

Even as I type this, tears stream down my face. My memories cause pain. I can still see certain images of my children and the deep pain and indescribable fear they endured. I can still hear the sound of their little feet scampering down the hallway of our house so many years ago as they ran from the terror they could hear through their parents' bedroom walls.

I know that because I chose to stay and they had no control over my decision, they must have felt an indescribable helplessness. Together, we kept this secret while walking on eggshells daily. My choice to stay was at the heart of where unforgiveness toward myself resided for years.

During the entire time I was in therapy with my first two counselors, forgiveness was never discussed. I actually worked with three counselors during the course of my healing journey. The first one helped me to call it what it is: abuse. The second one helped me to grow a backbone and finally say, "Enough!" And the third one walked me through the remainder of my journey, during which time I learned the essential value of choosing to forgive my abuser and, perhaps most importantly, to forgive myself.

Unforgiveness toward myself festered like a rotting sore, causing deep depression and isolation in my life. For a very long time, I believed I deserved the pain. After all, what kind of mother would allow her children to hurt the way I had? What kind of mother would allow her little boy to feel responsible to protect her from a six-foot-two gorilla of a man? What kind of mother would allow her children to see the horror they did and do little to nothing about it? All the while, I told my children I loved them every day, often multiple times in one day, and yet . . . I stayed.

I chose to forgive Ben. I also had to choose to forgive myself. Neither choice was easy. Neither choice came naturally. In fact, many times I've had to reflect back on that night I held hands with my youngest daughter and verbalized to God my decision to forgive, to release Ben into His hands, and to surrender my desire for justice. Since that night, I have witnessed the powerful influence that decision has had on my life. I would not be where I am today, free from the anger and all the emotions that nearly consumed me, had I not decided to forgive.

I hope that my messy story with all its painful memories will serve to encourage you. My desire is for you to know that forgiveness is truly possible and a vital step in your continued journey toward healing well and living free.

Understanding True Forgiveness

As you know by now, forgiveness is a significant part of the healing process. But inaccurate information on this subject can cause additional pain, set you on a major detour in your healing journey, and quite possibly derail you altogether.

Why is the pressure to forgive the all-too-common response when someone hears a victim of domestic violence share her story? Her story may make the listener feel uncomfortable, and they want to quickly put the matter to rest and move on. They don't know how to fix her, may even believe she brought it upon herself, and may harbor judgmental assumptions such as "Why didn't she just leave?" They tell her to "forgive and forget," as if somehow such a statement actually helps.

If I hadn't heard this sort of response as much as I have, I wouldn't be sharing it with you now.

Perhaps you have experienced this skewed advice as well. If you have, I want to extend a big, compassionate hug to you right now through my words on this page. If you have courageously shared your story and been told that all you need to do to make it all go away is forgive—please know it is simply not true.

There is a great deal about healthy forgiveness that often is largely misunderstood. A victim's beliefs in this area can and will impact her tremendously. Forgiveness is not a substitute for boundaries, nor should forgiveness eliminate consequences.

Rather, forgiveness is first and foremost for you. It is a decision you make by an act of your will. The decision to forgive is not driven by desire or feelings. When pain is involved, it will never feel "natural" to forgive. Instinctively, we want to defend ourselves, get back, and get even. We want those who hurt us to know they have done so and then make them pay. Bottom line, if you hurt me, I want to hurt you.

You may believe that by withholding forgiveness you are preventing yourself from experiencing any further pain and somehow protecting yourself. But this could not be further from the truth. Author Anne Lamott wrote, "In fact, not forgiving is like drinking rat poison and then waiting for the rat to die."[1]

You may think that by withholding forgiveness you are exerting some degree of control. In actuality, the very opposite is happening. Unforgiveness is about false control. Forgiveness is about freedom. I ask you, "Do you want false control, or do you want freedom?"

When you choose to let go of the right to get even or be repaid by your abuser for the pain he inflicted, profound healing at the deepest level will occur. If you wait on your abuser to take responsibility for his actions, your freedom will be held hostage. It sounds paradoxical, but actually, it is not. Withholding forgiveness keeps you entrapped in the pain. Living with unforgiveness is really self-inflicted imprisonment. When you refuse to forgive, you create invisible bars around yourself. Even after you have left your abuser, the effects of unforgiveness will rob you of the full benefits of your brave decision to leave.

The Value of Healthy Anger

I want to provide a word of caution here: be careful not to confuse feeling angry with thinking you have not fully forgiven your abuser. You can choose to forgive, employing all I described above, and still feel the emotion of anger. The fact that you feel anger, along with numerous other emotions, while continuing to journey forward is normal and actually quite healthy.

When I was still very engulfed in the throes of emotional pain, someone said to me, "Ramona, you're so angry. You need to stop being angry and move on." Her comment pierced me deeply. I felt so misunderstood and alone. The accusation and judgment behind her words seemed to inflame the already smoldering anger within me. Did she have any clue about the weight of the pain I carried? Did she care? Her "counsel" certainly did not bring me comfort or encouragement. If anything, it confused me and caused me to further isolate, not knowing whom I could trust.

Anger can be a very misunderstood emotion. Unfortunately, within some church communities, anger and sin are often viewed as synonymous. This interpretation of anger is not only wrong but also harmful. It is possible to be angry and not sin. The anger I'm referring to here is healthy anger. Healthy anger never abuses, attacks, or causes harm to oneself or others. Destructive anger expressed in this fashion is sin. (See appendix N for a comprehensive list describing healthy anger.)

We read in Matthew 21:12–13 how Jesus, upon entering the temple, became very angry with what He saw. "'It is written,' he said to them, 'My house will be called a house of prayer,' but you are making it 'a den of robbers.'" It angered Jesus to see how some people were taking financial advantage of those coming to worship. Anger was an appropriate response to this injustice.

Feeling the emotion of anger in response to sin is not sin. I felt anger for a long time, even after I made the decision to forgive Ben. This anger was a direct response to the abuse my children and I experienced. Anger was an appropriate and healthy response. It fit our situation. It also gave me the energy and wherewithal to continue pressing on through a very ugly and twisted divorce.

Anger can give us the energy we need for a season. It can help us accomplish difficult tasks. It can also help us purge the pain that could otherwise remain locked inside. In addition, anger is an integral part of grieving. Give yourself the permission to grieve. Allow yourself to fully feel and express your emotions. This is at the heart of what grieving well is all about. To heal well is to grieve well. You cannot have one without the other.

You will discover that as you permit yourself to fully grieve, your anger will slowly dissipate. Today I am free from the anger that once was so intense. I am grateful for my counselors who understood the value and the necessity of anger and encouraged me not to repress it. If you are not feeling anger, I suggest talking this over with your counselor. Perhaps you were not permitted to express anger as a child and likely were not allowed to show it in your relationship. That's why now it may be a struggle to feel and show healthy anger. But stuffing anger will hurt you in the long run. What matters is that you don't avoid your anger, minimize it, or feel shame because of it. Anger is a gift God gave you that allows you to grieve. You don't need to be afraid of it. Rather, grieving will allow you to feel it, and forgiveness will allow you to release it.

The Decision to Forgive

The decision to forgive is not something you *must* do; it is something you *get* to do. Once you truly understand that it is a gift you alone can give yourself, making this choice becomes empowering and not disempowering. Because of this, no one has the right to tell you when you "should forgive." The timing of this decision is exclusively up to you. Whoever the "they" may be in your life, "they" were not the recipient of the mistreatment and abuse.

Therefore, "they" do not have a right to decide when the timing is best for you.

Once you make the decision to forgive your abuser, don't be surprised when you find yourself having to reaffirm your decision. Your head and your heart may try to convince you that your prior decision was not real. This is precisely when you tell yourself, *I forgave him. I may not feel it. The pain and emotions I feel are still very strong. That's okay, because forgiveness is as much of a process as it is a decision.*

Let's look specifically at what forgiveness is and what it is not.

What Forgiveness Is Not

1. *Forgiveness will not magically change your abusive partner or heal your broken heart.*

   Forgiveness is something you do for yourself. It is important to realize that when you choose to forgive, there should be no strings attached. Meaning that, since your abuser has a free will, only he can decide whether he is going to change. Your decision to forgive him must be kept separate from his willingness or unwillingness to change. Forgiving someone is not a magic pill. Forgiving someone cannot override their will.

   Likewise, after you make the decision to forgive, the pain you feel will not just disappear. If that were the case, I think most people would jump at the opportunity to forgive! As my mother taught me when I was a young girl, if it's the right thing to do, it is seldom the easy thing to do. Granting forgiveness is not easy, but it is wise.

2. *Forgiveness does not mean forgetting.*

   Forgiveness definitely does not require that you forget all that happened to you. As a matter of fact, I hope you never totally forget. Your history is your story, and your story is a powerful reminder of how far you have come and how much you have grown. But reflecting on your history is not the same as morbidly dwelling on the pain of your past.

For me personally, glancing back at my "footprints in the sand" also serves to remind me that I was not alone. God was with me, carrying me, when I wanted to quit on myself and quit on life. Imagine if I had believed the misconception that to forgive means to forget? How would I have written this book? Forgetting is not only impossible but also dishonoring to yourself.

3. *Forgiveness does not mean accepting abuse.*
Some people think that if they forgive their abuser, they are somehow communicating the message that it was okay. This is not true! Recall with me the fact that forgiveness is about you, not about your abuser. Forgiveness never means saying that what happened to you was okay. Forgiveness does not make the other person right; it makes you free.

4. *Forgiveness does not require reconciliation to be real.*
The notion that to forgive requires that you reconcile with your abuser is not only erroneous but also dangerous. The idea that a victim of domestic violence must take her abuser back in order to demonstrate the sincerity of her forgiveness, simply put, is a lie. Seldom do we hear this kind of logic except in regard to the marital relationship.

Sadly, I have often heard this message communicated from those wearing the clerical collar. My question to those who give this faulty and unsafe advice is this: "If someone choked you, threatened to kill you, and called you names that would make a sailor blush, would you want to live under the same roof as that person?" Of course not!

Safety always takes precedence over idealism. And this includes emotional and verbal abuse too. The fact that a victim does not bear bruises others can see does not negate the validity of what she has suffered. Often the bruises of the heart take a lot longer to heal, and cause much deeper pain, than the black-and-blue marks that eventually fade away.

Reconciliation should occur only if there is verifiable and observable long-term change on the part of your abuser (see appendix I). And even then, the damage his abuse has caused to the relationship and your ability to trust him again may lead to a permanent severing of the relationship. Abuse always damages and often completely destroys a relationship. Without trust, there can be no relationship—at least not a healthy one.

What Forgiveness Is

1. *Forgiveness is freeing.*

   Holding on to unforgiveness will only keep you bound to the very person who broke your heart. It's not worth it. The cost to you physically, emotionally, and spiritually will be tremendous. If your true desire is to be free, you will need to wrestle with this difficult decision. I can assure you from my own personal experience that it's worth the struggle. Your ultimate freedom from the hold this pain has on you requires that you surrender it. And the only way to fully surrender it is through forgiveness.

   For me, I needed the comfort and the strength I have found only God can provide. Pain of this magnitude can feel insurmountable and beyond the reach of ever healing well. I encourage you, as you continue on your journey, to remain open to the true healing that only God can give.

   Even if you do not believe in God, or you are still working through questions about Him in the midst of your suffering, that's okay. But I do believe that He, more than anyone, wants you to *really* live. Just as I encouraged you in the introduction, "believe in my belief." Know that I believe for you and in you. I may never meet you, but I am praying for you. This is my promise to you and my gift.

2. *Forgiveness is healing.*

Each of us has a unique story, and you bear your own scars (even if they are not physical). Anyone who has experienced domestic violence knows that these relationships can be extremely complicated, and yet there is a common thread running through them: pain. Some of the pain is apparent to others; most is not. As you continue on your journey, the pain will subside in direct proportion to the healing that is taking place inside you.

Now is such a crucial time in your life. It is a new beginning, a new chapter. If your other chapters have not included God, I tenderly encourage you to remain open. He can and will use your pain for good, not only in your life but also in the lives of others suffering as you did. I'm living proof of this. If someone told me I would be writing a book on how to heal well and live free from the aftermath of domestic violence, I would have told them they were out of their mind! Yet I did. Today my life is a testimony of the power of God to bring healing to the deepest wounds only He can see as I partnered with Him in choosing to forgive.

3. *Forgiveness is loving yourself.*

As I mentioned before, many victims of domestic violence do not have a healthy love for themselves, or the experience of abuse has eroded away any love they did have for themselves. A huge part of the healing journey is learning to love yourself again. You are lovable. You are precious. You are beautiful. Despite what your abuser told you, *you are worthy of love.*

What you may not realize, however, is that loving yourself involves forgiveness—forgiving your abuser, forgiving those who have not believed your story or judged you in some way, and even forgiving yourself. As you walk through this process of forgiveness, the freedom and healing you will receive are a part of loving yourself.

The Key Is in Your Pocket

I have been able to write about the steps to healing well from domestic violence because I have *lived* the steps, each painful one. I have walked through them, just like you. Yet as I write this sentence, tears still flow. Although I know I have moved forward in a very healthy way in my life, the pain I still feel when I think about my kids lingers. I want to provide you with the know-how to heal fully and to move past the pain. Therefore, I believe that my transparency about this struggle will be far more helpful to you than anything else. I wish I could say forgiving yourself is easily accomplished, but I would not be telling you the truth. It simply is not.

If I desire complete freedom for you, my dear reader, I certainly desire the same for my children. I want my kids to be free. If you have children, you want the very same thing for them. But in order for our children to be free, we need to find freedom ourselves. We cannot give what we don't have. So working through forgiving yourself is an absolute necessity.

In working with women who have endured domestic violence, I hear the same thing from so many of them. "How can I possibly forgive myself?" For me, it was easier to forgive my abusive husband than it was to forgive myself. My biggest regret was staying as long as I did, resulting in my children seeing and hearing things they never should have. I ached and still do for the pain my children endured. As I type these words, I see the pictures of my precious children framed on the wall above my desk, their innocent little faces full of life and spunk. It wasn't fair to them. It wasn't fair at all.

The real irony, though, is that by not fully forgiving yourself, you will remain in bondage, and this in turn will affect your children too. Inadvertently, they will experience more pain. I believe this is because the connection between mother and child is solidified from conception. Even after the umbilical cord of life is severed, the bond remains. As a child feels their mother in the womb, so too can they feel her throughout their lives. I have also known those who were adopted or raised in a blended family and passionately attest to the bond they share with their mother. Truthfully, an umbilical cord is not what attaches mother to child but love does.

I also want to make sure I highlight a very important point. Forgiving yourself is a critical decision for you to make even if you do not have children. Each of us is valuable, and our value is not contingent on whether we are mothers. We all deserve the freedom that forgiveness provides.

After you have made the decision to forgive yourself, I encourage you to say it out loud. "I forgive myself." And then make it specific by saying, "I forgive myself for _____." I have found that talking out loud is very comforting because it is like I am having a dialogue with God. I believe He is the greatest listener. Plus, as crazy at it may sound, it's helpful for me to hear myself. As you have seen, I have had some pretty raw conversations with God.

If this approach isn't a good fit for you, then perhaps you may want to write out your decision to forgive yourself in your journal. Write it. Sign it. Date it. What matters is that you know you have crossed this line (when you said, "Enough!") leaving the iron ball (the abuse) behind, and you're now prepared to leave the chain (unforgiveness), too.

When you choose to forgive yourself, you release the need to feel guilty, to do penance, to shame yourself, or to hold on to any faulty beliefs that keep you trapped in the self-inflicted prison of unforgiveness. Forgiveness is the key that unlocks the prison door. It is not until you realize that the key has been in your pocket the entire time that you will reach through the bars, insert the key, and walk out free!

Honoring Your Children's Pain

This chapter on forgiveness would not be complete without addressing a crucial piece in the healing journey. Asking your children to forgive you.

What do I mean by this? If you have children who grew up around violence, whether physical, emotional, verbal, or however it was displayed, they are probably still carrying deep pain inside, regardless of whether they endured it for one day or for years. They may be in denial about it, but the pain will eventually surface in their lives, and they will be faced with the decision whether to address it or to bury it.

Approaching this issue requires extreme sensitivity on your part as well as the need to respect the individuality of each of your children. If you recall, forgiveness is both a decision and an ongoing process. This also holds true when you ask someone to forgive you. One child may need to hear you ask for forgiveness only one time. Another may need to hear you ask for forgiveness multiple times before they are able to truly hear and receive what you are saying. And with another child, it may take years for that child to be in a place where they will be ready to forgive you.

The point I am trying to make is that there is no formula for how or when to ask for forgiveness. Sensitivity to each of your children and where they may be at that moment in their lives is what this process is all about.

What's imperative is that they hear you taking genuine responsibility by acknowledging how your decisions or actions hurt them. It is your responsibility as their parent to honor their pain by asking for their forgiveness. Remember that you are asking for forgiveness, not requiring a response on their part. It's not your place to demand that they forgive you. Do not try to convince them that they "ought to" or "should" forgive you. This is their personal decision.

You do your part and give them the time, respect, and space to do theirs. Asking them to forgive you won't erase their pain, but it will give them a starting point from which to heal.

Even if your child chooses not to forgive you, as difficult as that may be, please do not feel guilty. You have done your part by opening the door regardless of whether they are currently ready to walk through it. Hopefully, sometime in the future, they will make this choice for themselves.

If your children were very young and not at an age where they were able to comprehend what was happening, you may find at some point when they grow up that you will need to address this matter. Just because your children were very young does not mean they were not affected by the abuse that went on in the home. The idea that children don't hear it or notice it is false. Of course they do. Even in utero a child can sense their mother's anxiety and other emotions that are a result of domestic violence.

I share the importance of asking your children to forgive you not to heap guilt on you—not at all. But if you forgive your abusive partner and you forgive yourself but you omit asking your children to forgive you, this is partial healing at best. It is when you extend forgiveness and also ask for forgiveness that healing well is truly possible.

In the same way that this was one of the most difficult chapters for me to write, you may have found that this has been one of the most difficult chapters for you to read. Often in life, it's the decisions we make by faith that require the greatest amount of fortitude. I encourage you to take the time to ponder the questions, pray the prayer, and receive the promises that follow this chapter.

Questions to Ponder

1. Prior to reading this chapter, did you hold certain ideas regarding forgiveness that you now realize are misconceptions? If so, what were they? How have these faulty beliefs about forgiveness affected you? What have others told you about forgiveness that has been hurtful or helpful?

2. After reading this chapter, do you believe you are in a place on your healing well journey where you are prepared to forgive your abuser? If not, what do you think is holding you back?

3. If you are ready to forgive your abuser, take the time to write a prayer or a statement of forgiveness that truly reflects what you think and feel. Remember that forgiveness is both a decision and a process. You get to set the pace. Do not permit others to determine this for you. If you are not yet ready to make this decision, what will help you get to that place?

4. Are you now ready to forgive yourself? Recall that forgiving yourself may take time and that you may never feel ready. Take the time to write down the things you need to forgive yourself for and then release them. If you are not yet ready to do this, what will help you get to that place?

5. If you have children, how do you think they may still struggle today from being exposed to domestic violence? Take the time to write down your thoughts regarding asking your children for their forgiveness. Remember, children are unique and may respond differently or need to be approached differently due to the sensitive and painful nature of this issue. There are no formulas. Just allow tenderness to be your guide when talking with them.

Prayer of Reflection

Jesus, please help me to understand the true meaning of forgiveness as You intended it to be. Clear up any confusion or faulty beliefs I have surrounding this issue. Give me discernment regarding the difference between forgiveness and reconciliation. I read in Your Word that we are to forgive, but I also know that forgiveness does not mean I need to trust this person again or take him back. Enable me to forgive and to surrender him into Your hands. You are my vindicator. You are my advocate. I realize that apart from You, it is humanly impossible to forgive him for the suffering he has inflicted. But with You all things are possible. Work in my heart so that I can begin this process of forgiveness.

Beyond forgiving my abuser, I ask You, Lord, to enable me to forgive myself. You are fully aware of my story. I do not have to explain myself to You, and I thank You for that. I want to be completely free. In order to be free, I must choose to forgive myself. My choice to be in this abusive relationship has hurt me as well as other people in my life. It hurts me to know this, but it also hurts me to hold on to unforgiveness toward myself. Help me, Jesus, to forgive myself.

Today, by an act of my will, I choose to forgive him (name of abuser), I choose to forgive myself, and I choose to forgive those (name them) who have misunderstood me and judged me without truly understanding my story. Thank You, Jesus, for the gift and example of forgiveness that You so freely gave to me on the cross. I receive Your forgiveness for myself as well as offer it from my heart to those who have hurt me.

And finally, Lord, please give me the sensitive discernment to know when it is best to approach each of my children to ask them to forgive me. I am no longer shaming myself for my decisions; however, I still recognize that my choices affected my innocent children. Hold them, Jesus. Heal them. Only You can use the pain they endured for greater good in their lives. Set them free to live their divine purpose with vitality and intention. Continue walking with them all the days of their lives keeping watch over them always. Amen.

God's Enduring Promises

O Lord, you are so good, so ready to forgive,
so full of unfailing love for all who ask for your help.
(Psalm 86:5 NLT)

In prayer there is a connection between what God does and what you do. You can't get forgiveness from God, for instance, without also forgiving others. If you refuse to do your part, you cut yourself off from God's part. (Matthew 6:14–15 Message)

And when you stand praying, if you hold anything against anyone, forgive them, so that your Father in heaven may forgive you your sins. (Mark 11:25)

Be kind and compassionate to one another, forgiving each other, just as in Christ God forgave you. (Ephesians 4:32)

And forgive us our sins,
as we have forgiven those who sin against us. (Matthew 6:12 NLT)

12

Your Gut Is Your Guide

Just recently, my son, my husband, and I decided to catch a movie. On a whim, it sounded like fun to treat ourselves to a fancy theater that offers reclining seats where you can order food right from your chair. This particular theater was for adults eighteen and older, so the added benefit was that we wouldn't risk the lovely experience of getting pegged in the head with popcorn thrown by rambunctious kids! Perhaps I'm showing my age, but nevertheless, you ought to try it. The comfy chairs alone sold me.

As we settled into our seats, I immediately took note of the emergency exit signs on both sides of the large theater screen. Definitely not something I paid any attention to when I was a kid. Funny how we notice different things as we get older. Had the fire alarm gone off in the middle of the movie, I would've grabbed the hands of my sweetie and my son and hightailed it out of there! But that's not what I did for many years when my internal alarm sounded. Instead, slowly over time, I ignored it altogether.

Your Internal Alarm

Your gut, or inner voice, is the alarm system inside you that warns you when there is danger. You were created with this internal alarm system to protect you and keep you safe. Imagine if I had heard the fire alarm go off and instead of heading out the emergency exit had just sat there continuing to watch the movie and eat my popcorn as the building burned down! Ignoring the alarm would not have kept the flames at bay. Eventually, you go down with the building if you don't exit before it's too late. Ignoring things does not make them go away. Ever.

"Everyone always told me I was so easygoing," Kate confided. "I just went along with what anyone else wanted to do. Truth was, after years of being told how stupid I was by my husband, I'd lost confidence in my ability to make even the simplest decisions. I could hear his voice in my head saying, 'You're such an idiot. How can you be so stupid?' I tried to tell myself he was wrong, but after hearing those kinds of messages for so long, I found it nearly impossible to shake them."

Reasons You Ignore Your Gut

Why do you ignore your gut? Great question. I think there are many reasons you do this. As with Kate in the example above, when your abuser continually demeans and shames you, over time you can begin to question your ability to make good decisions. Ultimately, this is a tactic to exert power and control. The more you begin to believe what he says about you, the more you doubt yourself, and the more you dial down the volume on your gut. Simply put, you stop trusting yourself.

I believe ignoring your gut directly results from the environment in which you are trying to survive. Crazy, abusive chaos is not conducive to objective thinking. As you continue living like this—ignoring your internal alarm system—your inner voice gets quieter and quieter. The demeaning and harmful things said toward you and about you eventually take a huge toll on your perception of yourself. You can be told "You're stupid, ugly, worthless, and crazy" for only so long before you believe it. Believing these lies results in diminished confidence and contributes to further isolation and dependence on your abuser.

While there are many reasons you end up ignoring your gut, I believe the bedrock reason is because you made the choice to value the relationship more than yourself. What you value most you prioritize most, regardless of what it is. Remember those super-traits? If, over time, you value keeping the family together more than keeping yourself safe, you will place all your energy and focus on the relationship. Faulty beliefs about yourself, marriage, God, commitment—I could go on and on—can all contribute to this very common yet dangerous response of turning down the volume on your gut. It's inevitable. To remain in an abusive relationship, you must slowly begin to dial down the volume on your internal alarm system. You cannot remain in a toxic, abusive situation and call it what it is at the same time. You will do one or the other, but you can't do both simultaneously.

A Broken Spirit

The more you believe the lies and the tighter you hold to faulty beliefs, including that the relationship is more important than your well-being, while ignoring your gut, the deeper you fall into a dark hole. Even if others may not be able to see it or sense your steady decline, it happens. Abuse breaks the spirit.

One afternoon while talking with Chelsey on the phone, I asked her, "What's wrong with me? I'm so sad all the time. I can hardly get out of bed. I walk around pretending things are okay. I fake a smile and just drive on, but inside I feel like collapsing. I choke back tears even while trying to do things like grocery shop. What's wrong with me, Chelsey?" I'll never forget her answer. She said matter-of-factly, "He broke your spirit."

A victim of domestic violence may be diagnosed with PTSD, depression, or anxiety, and any and all of these are quite fitting when one has been traumatized like this. But what I believe is at the core of your pain is a broken spirit. You won't find "broken spirit" in the *Diagnostic and Statistical Manual of Mental Disorders*. But it's what eventually happens as the gut is ignored and the abuse continues.

The Cost of Ignoring Your Gut

How do you ignore your gut? You ignore it by denying, minimizing, and rationalizing what you see and know to be true. Not only does this eventually lead to a broken spirit but it can also lead to a broken body. As I shared with you earlier, about ten years into my marriage to Ben, I was diagnosed with an autoimmune disease. No surprise to me now, although I did not see the writing on the wall back then. Your body and your emotional well-being cannot sustain prolonged mistreatment. You were created for peace, not turmoil. That's why listening to your gut is so crucial. When your gut goes "tilt" for too long, you can end up with physical ailments, depression, anxiety, and the formation of what is referred to as a "pseudo self." A pseudo self is what you become in order to survive what you ignore. In a sense, you risk losing your true self the longer you silence the voice within you. You don't consciously set out to create a false self. It happens in your quest to survive an abusive relationship. There is a high price to pay for ignoring your gut. The cost is losing your authentic self—and that is never worth it.

Turn It Back Up!

The great news is . . . if you were the one who turned the volume down on your gut, then you can be the one to turn it back up! I teach my clients exactly what I'm telling you right now. Turning the volume back up on your gut is not only possible but also essential to healing well.

You started doing this way back in chapter 3 by calling abuse what it is. Think with me for a second. How well would a broken arm heal if the doctor diagnosed it as diabetes? It wouldn't. So too by calling abuse anything other than what it is delays the healing process, perhaps even prevents it from ever getting started. This is not the case with the person who courageously calls it what it is and then follows through by saying emphatically, "Enough!" Even if you're uncertain regarding your next steps, calling abuse what it is, saying "No more. Enough!" and learning to honor your inner alarm system are all mandatory to moving forward and eventually being free.

I so appreciate my clients. I'm privileged to learn wonderful life lessons from them all the time. Sara's story is one of those "client nuggets" I treasure. I'll never forget something Sara shared with me in a session. We had been focusing on ways she could practice listening more to her gut. She said to me, "I remember when I first noticed I was starting to listen to my gut again. It sounds kind of silly, but I was in the produce section of the grocery store deliberating over which apples to select. It felt like all eyes were on me as I stood their debating over apple candidates. Then I remembered something you told me: 'Start with the little things, Sara. Deciding what you want in low-risk situations will help you get back in touch with your gut feelings. Be gentle with yourself. This takes time.' With that, I grabbed two shiny apples and one with a funny shape. I laugh now, but picking the funny-shaped one made me feel good inside. Maybe it's knowing that no one is perfect, not even an apple!"

Listening to your gut is about trusting it. The longer you've ignored it, the longer it may take you to begin hearing it again, that quiet voice inside encouraging you to believe that your life can be different, that you're worth every bit of the effort. Practicing, even in small ways like Sara, will eventually give way to an authentic confidence. This confidence will continue to grow as you honor your gut by no longer minimizing or ignoring what it's trying to tell you.

You *Do* Know

One of the most common phrases I hear from domestic violence survivors is, "I don't know." I assure them, "Yes, you do. You do know." The goal is not that you always make perfect decisions. Rather, it is that you learn to listen again and believe the voice inside you. It's that you sense deep down that life is not meant to be lived this way. You weren't created to be someone's punching bag—physically, verbally, emotionally, sexually, spiritually, or in any other way.

God created you to be cherished, to be protected, and to be loved. This way of living and being treated is not a bonus for a select few. It is intended for you too. Regardless of what you saw growing up or what you may have come to believe about how women are to be treated, the fact remains that you are God's precious, precious girl. He loves you and desires for you to be treated with respect, kindness, and safe love. **True love is safe love.** Anything apart from that is not genuine love. Genuine love cannot coexist with abuse. They are mutually exclusive. Once abuse enters a relationship, safe love ceases to exist. You deserve better. You deserve the real thing. But you must start with loving yourself. And loving yourself requires making tough decisions sometimes.

Your gut is a trustworthy alarm system. It's a gift you've been given. The more you continue to honor this gift by listening to it and following its lead, the stronger and clearer your inner voice will become and the stronger you will grow. Your growing confidence will directly parallel the degree to which you trust and listen to your gut.

"A few months into our relationship," Kate shared with the group, "I started to have this uneasy feeling inside. It felt like a knot in my stomach that wouldn't go away. I asked my boyfriend about it, and he told me, 'We're just getting to know each other. This is normal.' Now I realize that uneasiness I was feeling was my gut trying to warn me. Boy, I wish I had listened to it."

What has your gut been trying to tell you? Are you listening to it? You *do* know. Your gut is your gift. Trust it. Regardless of how long you've ignored it, or perhaps even silenced it, it's not too late to start listening to it.

Questions to Ponder

1. Thinking back, when do you believe you first started turning the volume down on your gut? If you recall, you do this by minimizing, rationalizing, or denying what you instinctively know to be true.

2. Where can you see evidence that you valued the relationship more than yourself?

3. What toll has your abuser's demeaning behavior and verbal assaults taken on you physically, emotionally, spiritually, or in other ways?

4. Do you see how a pseudo self has developed over time? How have you changed in order to survive or somehow try to manage the chaos in your private life?

5. What messages has your gut been trying to tell you? Are you ready and willing to begin turning the volume up on your gut by listening to it and starting to apply what it's telling you?

Prayer of Reflection

God, for so long now, I have ignored what I sense deep down inside. You made me with a built-in alarm system in order to protect myself from unsafe situations and unsafe people. For many reasons, some of which I don't totally understand yet, I have not listened to my gut. Please help me, Lord, to start to listen once again. Give me the courage and the strength to call it what it is and to stop denying or minimizing what's happening to me. I want to honor the gift of my gut that You have given me, but I don't quite trust myself anymore. Ignoring it has made it really hard to hear. I think I'm hearing it, but I'm not sure. Please make it clear to me. Please help me to distinguish between what is true and what is not. I feel so unsure of myself most of the time. I need You to heal the way I see myself and the faulty beliefs I have held on to.

My heart feels so injured and broken by the demeaning messages and abuse that I have lived with for so long. Heal my broken spirit and revive my ability to listen to my gut. I know You are the Spirit of truth who leads me into all truth. You use my inner voice to lead me. I trust that You can and will help me to respect and rely on this wonderful gift again. I am Your precious girl . . . even though I don't always feel this way and even though I struggle to believe it. Because I am Your girl, I can count on You. Thank You, God. I love You. Amen.

God's Enduring Promises

The LORD is close to the brokenhearted
and saves those who are crushed in spirit. (Psalm 34:18)

My eyes grow weak with sorrow;
they fail because of all my foes.
Away from me, all you who do evil,
for the LORD has heard my weeping.
The LORD has heard my cry for mercy;
the LORD accepts my prayer. (Psalm 6:7–9)

But you, God, see the trouble of the afflicted;
　　you consider their grief and take it in hand.
The victims commit themselves to you;
　　you are the helper of the fatherless. (Psalm 10:14)

I will praise the LORD, who counsels me;
　　even at night my heart instructs me.
I keep my eyes always on the LORD.
　　With him at my right hand, I will not be shaken. (Psalm
　　16:7–8)

I call on you, my God, for you will answer me;
　　turn your ear to me and hear my prayer.
Show me the wonders of your great love,
　　you who save by your right hand
　　those who take refuge in you from their foes.
Keep me as the apple of your eye;
　　hide me in the shadow of your wings. (Psalm 17:6–8)

13

Community—
Your Citadel of Choice

As a little girl, when I would hear a bump in the night, I'd crawl over to one of my younger brothers' rooms and whisper, "Hey, wanna sleep in my room tonight?" which really translated to, "I'm scared of the monster under my bed and will feel a whole lot safer if he eats us both!" My parents insisted we each sleep in our own rooms. They knew we'd giggle and keep each other awake, making us cranky, sleep-deprived kids the next day. This rule didn't stop me on those nights. I'd risk doing that military low crawl to one of their rooms knowing full well I was in deep doo-doo if Mom or Dad caught me! As silly as it may sound, what I was really seeking was community. A sense of safety in numbers. Protection because I was not alone.

There were no monsters under my childhood bed, of course. But that childhood desire for community—the desire for safety in the company of others—was a healthy and natural way to feel protected. And you can trust that desire, that gut feeling bubbling up in you today. Conversely, choosing to go it alone is not healthy or advisable.

Community . . . the Antidote to Isolation

Isolation is the breeding ground for abuse. Abuse will escalate over time when isolation is present. Community is the antidote to isolation. Community fosters accountability. Accountability enhances exposure, awareness, and protection for the victim.

> Isolation → Abuse Escalates
> *versus*
> Community → Accountability → Exposure,
> Awareness, and Protection

Ben's first physical assault happened in our third year of marriage. By that time, we had moved across the United States thousands of miles from our family and friends. When "things were bad," as I used to refer to it, I would avoid calling my family or reaching out to friends. Often Mom would call and say, "Hey, is everything okay out there? I haven't heard from you in a while." Typically, I allowed those messages to go straight to voice mail. I knew she was concerned, but I also knew I was not about to tell her what was really going on.

When an abuser's behaviors are exposed, the power and control he had in isolation can no longer work. Just as a wet blanket is to a flame, so is community to the abuser's antics. I believe one of the main reasons for this is that abusers are cowards. They are obviously bullies. And as we know, at the heart of every bully is a coward in hiding. Recall, the other term for domestic violence is intimate partner violence. An abuser almost always reserves his abusive behavior for his significant other or intimate partner. The same guy who leaves a nice tip for his female table server may go home and call his wife an ugly whore and pop her in the face. Only a coward would hit a woman. Only a lying coward would then deny it. Remember this.

The Many Faces of Community

Pursuing community is essential as you continue to heal well. We heal in community, not in isolation. Community is the kryptonite to secrecy, and secrecy is mandatory for isolation to remain in force. I cannot overemphasize how crucial it is for you to connect with healthy, well-informed resources. Community represents anything or anyone from a trusted, safe friend who encourages you to seek viable support to a knowledgeable, compassionate counselor who understands the nature of this complex issue to a support group in which women with similar histories share their stories and are supported.

Community can also include emotionally healthy family members who may not completely understand what you've been through but believe you. Be careful with this one though—family members who don't get it, don't want to get it, or have issues of their own that haven't been resolved may not be the best people to turn to. It's wonderful when you have family members who come alongside you during painful seasons in your life, but when family adds to your pain, that's not the best resource to rely on.

As you continue learning to trust your gut, pay attention to what it tells you regarding whom to trust as your community. I talked to God a lot as I began to reach out. Instinctively, I knew my heart was in a very vulnerable place and the last thing I needed was an insensitive person heaping additional shame on my already teetering avalanche of shame. So be careful when you reach out. Not everyone can be entrusted with your story. Many will not understand you or what you've been through. Ask God to lead you to the right and best people. Then trust the doors that open. (See appendix C for hotlines and resources.)

I realize that what I am encouraging you to do is not easy. I remember the first counselor I met with to discuss what was really happening behind closed doors. I was a nervous wreck walking into her office, but that day, sitting on the couch of a counselor who knew to call it abuse, was a true game changer for me. She requested that I fill out an abuse evaluation form detailing my experiences, and when I walked out of her office, something told me my life was about to change forever. Little did I know then that one day I would modify that abuse evaluation form and administer it to other victims of domestic violence. And I certainly never thought I'd write a book on the very topic I kept secret for so many years.

Don't Let It Happen Again

Community and accountability are so important because of this truth: experiencing and leaving an abusive relationship are not a sufficient guarantee it won't happen again. Let me say it one more time: just because you survived a painful relationship does not mean you won't land in another one. I have worked with many women, and the only thing that changed in their lives was the name of the abuser they were with. Changing your man will never change your life. Changing yourself will.

Kate's marriage of fourteen years to Andy was riddled with verbal and emotional abuse, with an occasional physical assault. Prior to her decision to file for divorce, she came to me for counseling. Then after a few months, she stopped coming to counseling. Two years later, she called me crying bitterly. I could hardly understand what she was trying to tell me. "I did it again, Dr. Ramona! I can't believe it. After all the hell I went through with Andy, I got into another relationship with a wolf in sheep's clothing. What's wrong with me? Why do I always seem to pick the monsters?"

Determine right now not to let this happen to you. You know your story. You've broken the silence and called it what it is. You've done the hard work of grieving, pursuing forgiveness, and learning to love yourself in a healthier way. When you connect with a healthy community, you decrease the likelihood of getting into another abusive relationship. All these intentional choices have a predictable outcome. A significant one is that the next time you decide to trust a man—whenever that might be—he will treat you with the dignity, respect, and safe love you deserve. And if he doesn't, you'll be strong enough, wise enough, and secure enough to say "Enough!" and continue moving forward.

Last Plug for Community

Intentionally seeking out and connecting with a trusted community is a wise and essential safeguard. Think of community as a type of citadel with which you surround yourself. In past times, a citadel was a castle or a fort that was used to protect the people of a city if they were attacked. Your emotionally healthy family members and friends, trained counselor, support group, and perhaps church family or synagogue together help to form this citadel in your life. Each entity provides not only a safe place for you to heal but also objective sets of eyes and ears when danger may be looming.

Not Following My Own Advice

Let me give you an example from my own life that will help to illustrate what I'm trying to say. My divorce took a long time, and not because we had any special assets we needed to divide in court. Rather, my former spouse dragged his heels in signing the paperwork. Once he realized that the ways in which he could leverage power and control were becoming fewer, he tapped into this last area and would conveniently not receive papers in the mail so he couldn't sign them. The excuses went on and on for six years. I believe another reason he delayed was because he knew I would not date until my divorce was final. I realize many people do begin dating once they are legally separated. I don't advise this for many reasons, but I definitely knew I personally wanted to wait for the divorce to be final. Plus, I really needed to focus on my children, who were hurting, angry, and confused in many ways.

After six years, the divorce decree finally came through, and I thought I was ready to move on with my life. Today I differentiate between "moving on" and "moving forward." I was clearly ready to *move on* after those six years were over, but I was most certainly not healed to the extent that I was ready to *move forward*. Moving on is about not looking back because you fear doing so will somehow keep you in that place. So you forge ahead. Moving forward is about looking back long enough to process what happened and to heal from the legitimate pain you suffered. Moving forward leads to healing well. Moving on leads to ignoring and minimizing, which keep you stuck in ways you may not even realize.

Now enter, stage right, the part of my story I was tempted to leave out. I made the commitment to you that I would be forthright and open with my story. I certainly cannot expect you to be if I'm not willing to be.

Just as the ink on my divorce decree dried, I opened myself up to a new relationship, thinking I was further along than I actually was. But I still hadn't learned to fully listen to my gut. It was screaming at me, "Don't do it! Don't go there! You will regret it!" Did I listen? No. Did it result in pain for many people, including myself? Yes, it did. Do I still feel remorse for my very unwise decision? I absolutely do.

The part I want you to hear is this: I was too vulnerable and too broken to make any rational or wise decisions regarding a new relationship. I thought because I had spent some time in counseling I knew what I was doing. I didn't. At least not fully. All of this could have been avoided if I had trusted the objective eyes and ears of my community.

In addition to ignoring my gut and minimizing my vulnerability, I totally blew off my dear friend Chelsey. She and I had been best friends for twenty-seven years at that point. Certainly, she had more than demonstrated her trustworthiness, but I foolishly downplayed it.

One evening we met at a little Italian restaurant for dinner. In the middle of the dinner, she got very quiet. Between the two of us, Chelsey is definitely the more reserved one. That in and of itself should have been enough to tell me, "Listen to her when she speaks." She looked up from her plate of linguine and said to me, "I'm really worried about you. Something about this relationship you're in just doesn't feel right to me."

My response to her was, "You don't know him like I do!"

It's a red flag when you start making comments like that! What matters is that your friend or concerned family member knows you and their gut is telling them danger is looming in your life.

At this point in our conversation, the tears really started to stream down Chelsey's face. Clearly, she was deeply concerned for me. She gave one last emphatic plea. She said, "Ramona, this relationship scares me!" at which point I bristled even more and pushed her concerns and her tears out of my mind.

How this hurts my heart still today. My response to my sweet BFF of so many years was wrong and unkind, and she did not deserve it. Thank God, she loves me unconditionally. Years later, as we talked about that night at the little Italian restaurant, I asked her to please forgive me. She was right. Very, very right.

When someone who loves you tells you they are concerned about the person you are seeing, please listen to them. You can avoid needless pain in your life, and you can protect those you love from enduring further pain caused by your choices. This is such an important issue. I truly hope you will receive and implement this counsel. There is no need for you to hurt anymore, at least not from self-inflicted pain. (Please refer to appendix O, "Red Flags," and appendix P, "Signs of a Bad Dating Choice," for additional insights.)

Red Flags: Don't Ignore the Stink!

I cannot emphasize enough how vital it is for you to recognize the red flags indicating you are tiptoeing around toxic territory, or that you may have already entered the wasteland of another unhealthy relationship. Either way, you must know these warning signs like you know the alphabet. Please do not be fooled into believing that only one red flag means you are somehow in safe territory. This is a huge mistake, one that can and will cost you dearly.

When clients tell me they are noticing only one red flag, which translates to, "So, Dr. Ramona, I can handle this; no need to over-react," I like to use a visual that quickly illustrates my point. I ask them, "If I promised to bake you my famous homemade brownies and bring them to our next session, would you be interested?" To this day, not one client has rejected my offer. Then I say, "I use only homemade, from-scratch ingredients, with one minor exception."

"What's that?" they quickly inquire.

"It's a little pinch of dog poo! Oh, don't worry. The brownies will be so delicious that you won't even notice it." How many takers do you think I have after I tell them that part? You're right. None!

My point is this: if you observe only one red flag, that's enough! If you don't actually see it but you *sense* it, that's enough too. You have come way too far to ignore your gut now. If you wouldn't eat a brownie that had just a hint of poo, why bite into a relationship that has indications of stink?

Knowing + Believing = Doing

Knowing the red flags is a must, but believing them is just as crucial. We can know something, but if we don't believe it, what we know will not affect what we do because there is no belief attached to it. We act on what we know only when we truly believe it. So believe the red flags. Believe the people who love you when they try to warn you something feels unsafe. You are learning to turn the volume up on your gut. You are in the process of doing this. You're not totally there yet.

As you remain committed to healing well, you will turn around someday and be the voice of wise counsel in someone else's life. Until then, believe the red flags when you sense or see even one. Trust your gut when it sounds an alarm. And receive wise counsel from whoever the "Chelsey" is in your life. Her wisdom and love were and still are a citadel in my life. I'm forever grateful for her love and friendship.

Community of all sorts is your protection, the walls of which will be your safeguard. Who's your citadel? Who will you allow to speak into your life? We all need people who love us with integrity and honestly speak into our lives. If you have someone like that, be thankful. If you do not, I encourage you to ask God to bring someone like this into your life. We are not created to live in isolation. We don't heal well in isolation.

We heal well only in community.

Questions to Ponder

1. How has the idea of community changed since the beginning of your relationship with your abuser? Have you become more isolated, over time losing contact with family and friends?

2. Look at the Isolation versus Community diagram in this chapter. To what extent have you seen this play out in your

life? How have you seen the connection between isolation and secrecy resulting in the escalation of abuse?

3. Reaching out to various forms of community requires tremendous courage. If you haven't already, are you willing to begin to connect with community now? List people and resources you believe would be trustworthy and safe options for you. Remember to pray for God's leading and trust the gut He's given you.

4. Leaving an abusive relationship does not immunize you from entering into another one. This is a faulty but common assumption. Therefore, are you willing to make the commitment to stay connected with a healthy community and to respectfully consider the input those in your community give you? Can you identify your possible blind spots that may impede you from receiving healthy feedback? If you aren't able to identify your blind spots, ask a trusted friend to be honest with you about what they foresee as potential future pitfalls. Your friend's feedback could ultimately save you from future pain.

5. After hearing my story of getting into a subsequent unhealthy dating relationship, do you recognize your own personal vulnerability in this area? What vulnerabilities can you identify?

6. Become familiar with the red flags listed in appendix O. Do you see any of these red flags in a relationship you may be considering or are currently in? Even if there's just one, what are your next action steps based on all you've learned up to this point?

Prayer of Reflection

Lord, I have lost contact with so many people in my life as I have isolated more and more. I want to connect with people again in an authentic and honest way. I don't want to keep this secret anymore. I have shared my story with a few, but I realize that in order to heal well and live free, I need to reach out and stay connected with a wider community. Help me to identify what this new community in my life will look like. I'm not sure whom I can trust. Please make it clear to me. Open the doors that are safe for me to walk through and keep the doors closed tightly that could cause my heart further injury. I know I have blind spots that increase my vulnerability. Protect me, Jesus. Show me areas within myself that have the potential of leading me down the wrong road. Help me to remain teachable and open to feedback from those who love me. And above all, please protect me from getting into another relationship with someone who will in the end mistreat me, abuse me, and leave me injured. I need You. Thank You for continuing to walk with me as we journey together. I am never alone with You by my side. I love You. Amen.

God's Enduring Promises

Two are better than one,
    because they have a good return for their labor:
If either of them falls down,
    one can help the other up.
But pity anyone who falls
    and has no one to help them up. . . .
Though one may be overpowered,
    two can defend themselves.
A cord of three strands is not quickly broken. (Ecclesiastes
    4:9–10, 12)

Without good direction, people lose their way;
    the more wise counsel you follow, the better your
        chances. (Proverbs 11:14 Message)

Fools are headstrong and do what they like;
> wise people take advice. (Proverbs 12:15 Message)

Plans fail for lack of counsel,
> but with many advisers they succeed. (Proverbs 15:22)

Help each other in troubles and problems. This is the kind of law Christ asks us to obey. (Galatians 6:2 NLV)

For where two or three gather in my name, there am I with them. (Matthew 18:20)

14

Free to Live, *Really* Live Again

I wish we were sitting together right now, because I'd give you
a big hug. What I'd want you to hear me say is this: You are
worth everything it takes to heal well. It may be hard to see
now, but healing well rather than merely moving on is one of the
greatest decisions you'll ever make. The wonderful news is that
this decision has built-in rewards that will continue to unfold in
your life over time. Take a moment to reflect on this. You *are* worth
it. You are so precious. I know this is true without ever meeting
you. And although I may never know the details of your particular
story, I know what brought you here.

Your pain brought you here.

This is the divine juncture where miracles happen. Miracles
occur at the precise point where pain meets promise. Promise can
be summed up in one word: love. God is love (1 John 4:16), and He
holds the promise. Because of His love for you, He yearns for you
to live, *really* live. That's the promise part. He tells us He has come
so we may have life and life more abundantly (John 10:10). Abundant life doesn't mean pain-free life. But it does mean abuse-free
life. Abundant living allows us to live beyond our circumstances.

By acknowledging your pain, feeling your pain, and learning from your pain, you can experience what it means to live abundantly and not in servitude to your pain.

Scraping your way through life, wearing a dozen masks just to get through the day, is not God's desire for you. You are precious because you are His. He loves you beyond comprehension. His love for you is not based on whether you believe in it or feel it. The truth is when you aren't able to believe in or feel His love for you, He continues to pursue you with His whole heart. He knows your story more than anyone. And no matter who else believes you, God does.

God Sees YOU

Often after an abusive blowup in our home, I'd gather the kids together and we'd climb on top of one of our beds. Typically, we'd hold hands, cry, and talk to Jesus, but many times before praying, I would tell them that God sees us. I'd explain that God was very aware of everything that was happening. I would tell them that somehow God was going to help us. Even though I wasn't sure how at the time, I believed it. In my desperation to comfort my kids as well as myself, that's what I said. My sincere intention was to give them hope in exchange for the fear and despair we all felt. In the deepest recesses of my very dialed-down gut, I believed there was an end in sight. I just didn't know how to get there yet.

I was shocked when many years later I discovered that "the God who sees me" is an actual name for God! The name in Hebrew is *El Roi* (EL raw-EE). You can find it in the first book of the Bible, Genesis 16:13. It blew me away when I learned this! So much so that I decided to have *El Roi* tattooed in Hebrew on my forearm as a reminder that God really does see us, especially in our pain.

Even though I do not know the details of your situation, God does. And He does not have favorites. His desire for me to truly live and enjoy life is the same desire He has for you. None of us has to earn it. We just have to receive it. This is a simple truth but definitely not an easy one to apply to ourselves, especially after abuse has left its imprint on our self-perception.

I can recall, like it was yesterday, taking my kids to school, swim or soccer practice and arriving at their destination not able to recollect how we got there—and I was the driver! My mind and emotions seemed to be strapped to the front cart of a roller coaster going up, down, and all around, but with no end in sight. When things were good, I was good. But, when things were bad, nothing was good. Living in an abusive relationship will always feel like you're on a roller coaster. When you're struggling simply to survive day to day in what feels like an endless pit of relationship despair, the thought that God loves you and wants you to enjoy life can seem like a tease at best. The truth is no one holds more value in God's eyes than anyone else. I am no more deserving of God's love than you are. Just as He saw me in my pain, He sees you in yours.

It's Possible for You Too

Many years ago, while I was still entangled in the cycle of abuse, Elle, a precious friend of mine, invited me to accompany her to a church a few hours from where we lived. This particular friend is one of the sweetest, kindest individuals I have ever known. Her gentle but persistent encouragement to join her persuaded me to go. I had no idea what I was in for, but afterward I was so grateful I did not miss what God had in store. Funny how we seldom realize He is at work behind the scenes while we're in the midst of whatever seems to be holding us captive.

Elle explained to me that this church had a unique prophetic ministry. I was desperate for anything at that point. I thought I would hear how God was going to save my marriage. After all, that's what I had asked Him to do for so many years.

After we arrived, I quickly sensed that the people at this church were genuine and loving. We were told that if a prophecy spoken over us was truly from God, it would happen in due time—not our time but His time. They also explained about the role of free choice. We can hear a prophecy that is from God but ultimately miss out on it because we opt not to do our part.

In the same way, people have a choice whether to heal and grow from the pain they experienced. Some will opt to remain in the pain, never actualizing complete freedom in their lives. Others, like you, will pursue freedom and do whatever it takes to get there. But remember that the healing well journey involves progress, not perfection. Since the residual effects of trauma do not simply go away with time, you may experience triggers and grief-like feelings long after you leave the abusive relationship. This is not unusual and not a reason to panic. If anything, these moments are opportunities to be tender with yourself and remind yourself how far you've come.

As I waited, two women approached me and asked if they could pray with me. I eagerly agreed, but I was nervous. My hands were sweaty, and my heart was beating fast. When they started to prophesy, I could feel the sweet presence of the Lord, not in an emotional sort of way but in a *this is real* sort of way. It's hard to explain, but I could feel Jesus's presence as if He were standing right next to us. While I can't recall everything the women said, two particular phrases have stayed with me to this day. "God desires that you live, *really* live!" one of them said. The other added, "He will resurrect what is dead in your life." I can't begin to explain how much I wanted this prophecy to be true. And it aligned with what I knew Scripture promises us.

But I thought, *Live, really live? Really?* Taking a quick mental assessment of how much my life was in complete shambles, I questioned the validity behind what was said. Honestly? God wanted me to not just scrape my way through life but truly enjoy it? I knew if this word was from Him, there would be no denying it when it happened. It would require a miracle because inside I felt dead. And my marriage was in cardiac arrest.

When I heard that God was going to resurrect what was dead in my life, my immediate thought was that God was going to resuscitate my marriage. Like most victims of domestic violence, I couldn't imagine He was talking about me! Of course not. My whole focus and all my energy went toward saving my marriage. It didn't occur to me that God's intention was to resurrect all that the abuse had killed inside me. It can take a very long time to begin factoring yourself and your well-being into the possibility the miracle will happen *for you* and *in you*.

Most of the nights back then I spent crying myself to sleep. The majority of our pillowcases had mascara stains from the tears that never seemed to stop, especially in the stillness of the night. *Live, really* live? Was it even possible? Was it possible for me?

Yes!

And it is God's passionate desire for you too!

He wants you to live, *really* live! You continue doing your part, and He will do his. Yours is the part you can do something about— what you can work on, what you can learn, what you can let go of. God's part resides in the impossible, the realm of taking you out of your pit of relationship despair and placing you in your own unique promised land. His part is healing the broken places inside you (and your children) that only He can see. And only He can heal. If this hadn't happened for me, I would struggle to believe it too. But as I look back over the years and see the healing He has brought about, I can emphatically say it has happened. And I wholeheartedly believe it can and will happen for you too.

I'm still believing for you as I promised at the beginning of this book. You are learning to believe again for yourself. Your ability to believe again is slowly returning. Don't doubt this based on what you feel from day to day. Know it is true because you have intentionally chosen to heal well and live free. Remember, you are not simply moving on; you are moving forward with intention. Let's take a look at what results from moving forward with intention.

Thriving beyond Abuse

There are many helpful books out there on the topic of domestic violence, and most of them talk about moving from victim to survivor. I agree that healing well involves both of these phases. However, I propose that there is a third phase, a continued opportunity for growth that goes beyond survivor.

There is a distinct difference between living and *really* living. The former (living) is to survive an abusive relationship. The latter (*really* living) is to thrive beyond it. When we make the conscious decision to heal well, we move from survivor to overcomer. This is where *really* living begins to blossom. A survivor lives beyond the abuse, which is incredible in and of itself. But an overcomer learns how to thrive and *really* live. I have met many heroic survivors who have committed to the healing well process and today are living, *really* living. They are overcomers in every sense of the word.

I want to add a very important caveat—it is just as imperative to recognize that you have been victimized as it is to survive and move beyond victimization. You can technically leave an abusive relationship (i.e., be a survivor), but if you do not acknowledge that you were a victim, you will never be able to fully heal well and live free. You cannot heal to the point of being an overcomer until you have first acknowledged you were a victim.

I have worked with clients who really struggled saying the "v" word (to quote them). They thought accepting the fact that they were victims somehow meant they were weak. Being a victim does not mean you are weak. It just means you were a victim.

"I can't stand to think I was a victim!" Sara said with disgust as she sat with her arms crossed on the couch in my office. "It makes me feel weak and foolish. Even with all I now understand about relationship abuse, it's still really hard for me."

I responded by gently asking, "Remember when you shared with me about your friend who was raped? Would you agree she was victimized?"

Without hesitation, Sara answered, "Of course I would, in a heartbeat!"

"So does that make her weak?" I continued.

"Of course not!" Sara replied incredulously.

"Remember, Sara, domestic violence is a crime just like rape is a crime. Being victimized is not synonymous with being weak. Nor does it imply you will remain a victim. This is a great place to start being more tender with yourself. Reaching out for support is one of the first steps survivors do. Be patient with yourself and remember how far you've already come."

Being a victim of a crime does not imply weakness. It simply means something was perpetrated against you. Calling it what it is, and domestic violence *is* a crime, places the responsibility of the crime on the perpetrator...where it belongs. There is never an excuse for abuse. And the victim of any form of crime is never responsible for the criminal act that took place against them.

Granted, when I think back on my former marriage, I see ways in which I could have handled things better or responded in a more mature fashion. Possibly, you do too. However, taking responsibility for your choices is not the same as taking responsibility for your abuser's. Furthermore, acknowledging the fact I could have handled certain matters better does not imply that by doing so I could have stopped Ben from acting abusively. Ben behaved that way because he chose to, not because I caused him to. Solidifying this distinction regarding who is responsible for what is critical.

Now let's take a closer look at what it means to be an overcomer. The healing well and living free journey is a process, as the diagram shows:

Victim	→	Survivor	→	Overcomer
(Lives in abuse) →		(Lives beyond abuse) →		(Lives, *really* lives)

Note: The amount of time spent progressing through each phase will be unique to each person.

It's important to understand that a survivor who has not worked through all the steps essential to healing well can still struggle with shame, unforgiveness, trusting herself again, and staying connected to a healthy support system. As a result, she will get stuck in the healing process. Each of the steps in the previous chapters are important to heal well and live free. An overcomer makes the decision to walk the entire process regardless of how long it takes or how difficult it may be.

Overcomers continue to learn and apply what it means to truly love themselves in a healthy way. For a long time, your energy and focus were on helping your abuser change. Now you may find that your focus is on helping your children heal, which is important, but this is still not enough. Intentionally focusing on what you need, what you enjoy, or what puts a spring in your step is loving yourself. And this is very important.

One of my clients received a beautiful gift from a dear friend. "At first I was shy about it. I didn't even take it out of the gift bag for several days. But when I realized I could carry the Coach purse and not feel guilty and nobody was going to question why I would have such a nice thing, I knew I was beginning to understand what it means to love myself." She continued, "It might sound silly, but accepting I could carry an expensive purse made me feel good inside."

Loving yourself even in the simplest of ways contributes to thriving beyond abuse. Your abuser may have falsely led you to believe you're not worth it. But loving yourself says you are. These baby steps in your thinking process will take you beyond surviving and catapult you into thriving, where the miracle of living, *really* living begins.

Your Pain Is Not for Naught

What is it you are really hoping for?

Besides the understandable desire to put the pieces of your life back together again and experience genuine joy and peace, what I believe resides at the heart of most who endure relationship trauma and loss is the hope that their pain was not for naught. A survivor is thankful to no longer be a victim but an overcomer craves more than survival. An overcomer wants to ensure their pain was not wasted, that there can be purpose in it, that it can and will be used to help others who are walking through that same dark place where they once were.

A couple weeks later, Sara and I met again. This time I noticed a new bounce in her step when she arrived. She barely sat down before excitedly sharing, "Our last conversation really left me thinking. I've spent hours journaling on what we talked about. I wanted to understand why I had such a tough time recognizing my own personal victimization. When you suggested being tender with myself, it really struck a chord with me. I have thought about what you said, and I realize being tender and compassionate with myself is a way I can love myself. My pain was real, and it still hurts when I reflect back. But I don't want my pain to be wasted. I want to be able to fully heal so I can help others, and I've come to see that realizing I was a victim is an important step in that process. It's amazing how freeing that has been for me."

Pay It Forward

As an overcomer, you will at some point choose to share what you are learning with those who desire to listen. You will recognize that your story is a tribute to all God has done with the brokenness in your life. Equally important, you will acknowledge the part you played in remaining committed to yourself. Both God's part and your part together will result in the person you are becoming—your strongest self. That's something worth celebrating!

Why does an overcomer share their story? Because the gratitude and joy they feel about their decision to heal well and live free is not something that can be contained. Sharing your story, however, happens on no one's timetable but your own. For me, it took many years before I said much at all. Personally, I had to do a lot of work on my erroneous belief that I needed to appear perfect and have it all together. Remember, I am a marriage and family therapist. Divorce due to battery and adultery doesn't make for a great marketing campaign!

Guarding Your Heart

Learning to love myself, by accepting myself, imperfections and all, while also learning to distinguish between what I could control and what I couldn't, eventually led to the freedom to unashamedly share my story.

Many of us resist the idea of sharing these sensitive parts of our lives. Because we were hurt so deeply, we become guarded. For a very long time, I lived guarded because I didn't know whom I could trust, and I certainly didn't trust myself yet either. So I hid, always fearful others could see I was pretending on so many levels.

As I worked with my counselor, attended a support group, and read anything I could get my hands on pertaining to this topic, I discovered that there is a difference between guarding our hearts (Proverbs 4:23) and living guarded. Guarding our hearts is wise.

It simply means we don't entrust ourselves or our stories to those who have not demonstrated they are trustworthy.

Knowing the difference between living guarded and guarding your heart doesn't happen overnight. So although as an overcomer you will eventually reach the place where you can comfortably share your experience with trustworthy people, doing so will take time. Remain sensitive to the pace that suits you best while guarding your heart along the way.

Gratitude: Your GPS

Gratitude is the key to maintaining an overcomer's mind-set, and gratitude is central to remaining committed to your journey. Choosing and maintaining gratitude will keep you on the healing well trajectory. Regardless of which juncture you are currently at, gratitude for the ground you've gained will keep you walking your path.

Gratitude for how far you've come will also give you a desire to share your new understanding of yourself, your life, and your choices with another wounded sojourner. You're doing more than moving on. You're moving forward. One of the ways an overcomer continues to move forward is by taking the hand of another and encouraging her to believe that she too can heal well and live free. Remember, until a victim or a survivor can believe it for herself, she can believe in *your* belief for her.

What's Ahead?

As this chapter comes to a close, I have some wonderful news for you. When you commit to this journey, you give yourself a gift so astounding that I struggle to put it into words. Here's the great news: your decision to heal well will inevitably result in the very best years of your life unfolding before you. You heard me right. Your best days are ahead of you, not behind you. This does not mean you will never have any problems or never experience hurt or loss in your life. What it does mean is that as you live, *really* live, you will experience the freedom for which all of us were created: "It is for freedom that Christ has set us free" (Galatians 5:1). Even if you still struggle to believe this, it doesn't make it less true. I may not believe gravity is true, but if I jump off the roof, I'm still going to splat! Not believing something does not negate its validity. It just indicates you aren't quite there yet. That's okay. Even at chapter 14, it's okay.

I want to interject one additional observation you may not be aware of. It is possible not everyone is going to applaud the new you. Those who were able to leverage the broken, poor self-image, minimize-my-needs you will often resist the healthy changes you are making. View this as a compliment and allow their objections to be the very fuel you need to press on. Furthermore, don't allow your continued growth to be stunted because your kids may not be there yet. You have to keep moving forward even if others (including your kids) get stuck. The best thing you can do for those you love is to get unstuck and remain unstuck. That's what you're doing. The message you will send your kids is, "If Mom can do it, you can too!"

Be assured, your commitment to heal well will always translate into something positive. You are learning to trust your gut more. You are able to recognize red flags. You are no longer keeping a secret. You know the value of staying connected with a healthy community. You are working through the delicate decision and process of forgiving. You are helping others to see there is hope for them too. You are laying down your masks one by one and daily learning to love yourself authentically and tenderly. All of this can be summed up in one word: Overcomer!

You may not have realized it, but what you were really hoping for when you picked up this book was to find a way to heal so authentically and profoundly that your life would never be the same again. Your best days are ahead of you.

Questions to Ponder

1. What were your first thoughts after reading the title of this chapter? Has it ever occurred to you there is a distinct difference between living and *really* living? Where do you see yourself on this continuum?

2. As you have progressed through this book, what thoughts and feelings have been stirred whenever you have heard me say God loves you? He sees you? He's aware of your pain? Has knowing that *El Roi*, "the God who sees me," is an actual name for God affected in any way your perception of God regarding your personal story?

3. Have you been able to acknowledge you were a victim of domestic violence? What are your beliefs surrounding this term? Have you been willing to extend compassion toward yourself and separate your abuser's responsibility from your own? (Please reread the section "Thriving beyond Abuse" if you're still blaming yourself for the abuse.)

4. After reading about the phases of healing well and living free (from victim to survivor to overcomer), where do you believe you currently are in your healing well journey? What do you think will help you move to the next phase? What do you believe may be holding you back? If you are in the overcomer phase, what are you enjoying most about this?

5. Why do you believe you started reading this book? What are you *really* hoping for? What will it require for you to attain it?

6. When you live, *really* live, the best years of your life await you. What desires do you have for yourself in the next chapters of your life?

Prayer of Reflection

Hearing the phrase "live, really live" stirs so many emotions and thoughts within me. I earnestly want to believe this is possible in my life, but I still find myself struggling to imagine it will ever fully come to pass. Thank You, Jesus, for tenderly loving me through this journey. So many times I've wanted to give up. I've wanted to say, "It's too hard." But each time I felt You gently nudging me onward. I am moving forward and not merely moving on. I also realize that without You encouraging me to take each step, I'd never make it. Help me when I falter. Help me when I can't see the way before me, let alone the possibility of living, really living.

The concept of an overcomer is hard for me to wrap my mind around. It sounds good, and I think I want this, but I'm not sure I have the strength to persevere. You, Jesus, are the ultimate overcomer! You know what it means to overcome and exactly what it requires to attain it. Only through You will this transpire in my life. I am so incredibly grateful for Your unconditional love for me. I have lived with conditional love for most of my life. Only when I met You did I realize I can be loved and accepted just as I am. I desire to continue along the path of healing well and living free. Thank You for this gift. Thank You for setting me free. Amen.

God's Enduring Promises

You gave me life and showed me your unfailing love.
My life was preserved by your care. (Job 10:12 NLT)

Guard your heart above all else,
for it determines the course of your life. (Proverbs 4:23 NLT)

Christ has set us free to live a free life. So take your stand! Never again let anyone put a harness of slavery on you. (Galatians 5:1 Message)

She gave this name to the LORD who spoke to her: "You are the God who sees me," for she said, "I have now seen the One who sees me." (Genesis 16:13)

The thief comes only to steal and kill and destroy; I came that they may have life, and have it abundantly. (John 10:10 NASB)

Come to me, all you who are weary and burdened, and I will give you rest. Take my yoke upon you and learn from me, for I am gentle and humble in heart, and you will find rest for your souls. For my yoke is easy and my burden is light. (Matthew 11:28–30)

> You will keep in perfect peace
> all who trust in you,
> all whose thoughts are fixed on you! (Isaiah 26:3 NLT)

15

Free to Love, *Really* Love Again

Is it even possible to love again?

Leaving an abusive relationship can feel like crawling off a battlefield. Your heart is tattered. You're depleted. Few may believe or know all you went through. The idea of ever loving again, *really* loving, where your body, heart, and soul are truly safe, seems inconceivable for most survivors.

I'd intended for my marriage to last a lifetime. My white-knuckled commitment to that marriage could have potentially cost me my life—if not my physical one, certainly my emotional one. Nothing is worth that. Nothing.

Just as we learned that we can live *or* live, *really* live; likewise, we can love *or* love, *really* love. I thought I was doing both prior to walking my own healing journey. I certainly was trying. What I have come to understand is I was not experiencing either. In this final chapter, I want to share with you what I believe is loving and being loved in its fullest sense. This understanding has changed me and the way I love and receive love in such a profound way, this message would be incomplete if I did not pass it on to you.

Loving yourself, based on an accurate understanding of God's love for you, and allowing this understanding to free you to give and receive healthy love with others are the natural by-products of healing well. They are also the apex of living free.

You may think you already do love others. I have no doubt you have some beautiful, loving relationships in your life. For example, I loved my best friend, Chelsey, and she loved me. But because I didn't have a healthy love for myself, I was not free to love her as deeply as I do today. The kind of love I'm talking about cannot happen when abuse of any kind is running in the background. In other words, it's impossible to have a healthy love for yourself while at the same time allowing yourself to be abused. And a healthy love for yourself is critical for love to fully flourish in any relationship.

Treat Yourself to Normal

When I was steeped in the abuse and even after the relationship was over, I was so wounded and confused about love that even loving my family and friends was not all it could be. The residual effects of abuse do not automatically stop after you leave. Therefore, to experience all that healing well and living free entails, you must acquire an accurate, truth-based understanding of love. Only after you have this understanding are you free to love, *really* love again.

I learned this myself in a very unexpected way. One afternoon I came home and saw that my youngest daughter had written the following message in lipstick on the bathroom mirror: "Mama, why not treat yourself to normal?" In a few strokes, she reminded me I'm worth it. I'm valuable. I deserve to be treated with safe, kind, truth-based love. This child has a way with words like few people I know. She doesn't beat around the bush, ever! I love that about her even though sometimes it's hard to hear what she has to say. But I've never doubted that it is pure love for me that motivates her.

I left her lipstick-penned words on the mirror for months. I needed the daily reminder at that time. Whenever I struggled, I would read her words, always secretly hoping her message would become my reality.

What did my daughter mean by normal? She meant I needed a *new* normal. She desperately wanted me to raise the bar in my life from the normal I once knew to a new normal, which I would reach only by intentionally working on myself. From the mouths of babes for sure. Her direct honesty was and is such a gift to me.

Am I Lovable?

Loving yourself is not the same thing as narcissism. Narcissism is about being *in love* with yourself. This term comes from a story in Greek mythology in which the young Narcissus fell in love with his own image reflected in a pool of water. This is not at all what I'm talking about here. For me, the only way I have been able to develop a healthy love for myself has been through wrestling with the questions "Am I truly lovable?" and if I am, "Why?"

Think about this for a second. Seriously. Put the book down and ask yourself these two questions:

"Am I lovable?

"Why am I lovable?"

The first question speaks to our *value*. The second question speaks to our *belief*. We love what we place value on. We value what we believe holds worth.

When I allowed Ben to call me names early on in our dating relationship, this was a clear indication that my love for myself was skewed. The name-calling happened way before the physical assaults. This is typically the case in abusive relationships, not always but typically. Regardless of whether he was bruising my heart or bruising my body, by allowing Ben to treat me in this manner, I was definitely not loving or valuing myself. No matter how many times he said he loved me, emotionally healthy love does not abuse its beloved.

The truth of the matter was I did not really love or value myself. I thought I did, but I didn't. I lived like that for a very long time. If someone had asked me, "Do you love yourself?" back then I would have said, "Yes." But I would have been wrong and grossly misguided. For many years, I knew what to say, but I just didn't really believe it down deep. It wasn't until I had this point of reckoning with myself that my life began to turn the bend.

Certainly, by now you have recognized that my faith is central in my life. However, even my faith was messed up for a long time. My perception of God was so screwed up that it affected how I lived in relationship with myself and with others. Early on, I saw God as Someone who was just waiting to pounce on me when I wasn't perfect. I wasn't attracted to the idea of "being in relationship with Him," as some of my sweet church friends would suggest. I was a diehard perfectionist who didn't want the added strain of trying to please a perfect God. Boy, was I deceived. Self-deceived.

Thank God I'm not God. I would have certainly condemned myself. But He didn't. He doesn't think like we think. In my wrestling, I asked the tough questions, one of which was "Am I truly valued by God?" Either I am or I'm not. I ran from God for a long time due to my faulty perceptions of Him. Even though I deeply desired to be close to Him, I was afraid to fully trust Him and even more afraid to believe I was loved by Him.

The turning point came when I simply decided to believe it. It really was that simple. I came across a verse that said, "Whoever does not love does not know God, because God is love" (1 John 4:8). Read the sentence like this: "Whoever does not love *herself* does not know God, because God is love." How can I love myself if my perception of God is skewed? I can't. Neither can you.

There is not a single person on this planet who can slip their name into God's position. Ramona is love? Nope. Ramona can learn to love herself and others in the way she was created to love only *after* she learns to receive God's perfect, unconditional love for her. This is where healthy love must begin. It has to begin with Love itself. Only God *is* love. Until we embrace this, we will never fully experience the zenith of love.

I realize some of you may have a list as long as your arm of reasons why you resist God's love for you. I am not minimizing your why's, I'm only encouraging you to examine them. Are your reasons for keeping God at bay actually helping you? Do you feel better by keeping Him out of your life? Or perhaps you're compartmentalizing God by tucking Him nice and neatly into a Sunday church service box, not allowing Him to be a part of the rest of your days. For me, I had to separate the erroneous messages I heard and believed from what was really true. Perhaps you do too. The truth is that He loves you. And because He loves you, you can choose to love yourself.

But how?

The answer is when you understand and accept the way God loves, then you can extend that love to yourself.

The Litmus Test for Real Love

I want to share with you what I believe is the litmus test for love. It has dramatically altered how I now understand love. It's found in 1 Corinthians 13:4–8. You may have heard this passage read at weddings, or perhaps you've heard it taught from the pulpit. I don't believe there is any other descriptor of love as perfect as this one.

> Love is patient, love is kind. It does not envy, it does not boast, it is not proud. It does not dishonor others, it is not self-seeking, it is not easily angered, it keeps no record of wrongs. Love does not delight in evil but rejoices with the truth. It always protects, always trusts, always hopes, always perseveres. Love never fails.

Since God *is* love, replace the word *God* wherever the word *love* appears.

God is patient, God is kind. God does not envy, God does not boast, God is not proud. God does not dishonor others, God is not self-seeking, God is not easily angered, God keeps no record of wrongs. God does not delight in evil but rejoices with the truth. God always protects, always trusts, always hopes, always perseveres. God never fails.

This is who He is. This is the essence of His being. This is His heart for you. With all my heart, I implore you to open yours. You have been robbed of real love for long enough. Please do not allow another day to pass without receiving His. Even if you've warmed a pew for years, your view of God can still be off track. Regardless of where you are, this can be your turning point too.

As you understand God's love for you, you will be able to stop shaming yourself, judging yourself, and holding on to unforgiveness toward yourself. When you allow His love in, it will reach down to the deepest recesses of your being and begin to do its work. His love can heal what people can't, a book can't, a pill can't, a bottle can't, a drug can't, falling in love with another person can't. Only His love can heal you well so you can live free.

Reflect on this. Take as much time as you need. Go for a walk. Take a long bath. Really ponder what you just read. Pick the book back up only after you've allowed yourself ample time to reflect on and receive this message. This message is at the heart of this book. It's the golden nugget that will change your life. I promise.

Now let's pursue this a little bit further. Wherever you see the word *God* in the above verses, replace it with your own name.

_____ is patient (with herself), _____ is kind (toward herself). _____ does not envy (or compare herself with others), _____ does not boast (in her own abilities without giving recognition to God), _____ is not proud (meaning arrogant). _____ does not dishonor others (or herself), _____ is not self-seeking (attempting to live her life apart from God), _____ is not easily angered (with herself), _____ keeps no record of wrongs (when she blows it). _____ does not delight in evil but rejoices with the truth (she chooses to believe the best about herself, not demanding unrealistic perfection). _____ always protects (herself physically, emotionally, spiritually, and in every other way), _____ always trusts (her gut and utilizes wise counsel from those who truly have her best interest in mind), _____ always hopes (knowing God will work all things for her good even though not all things are good), _____ always perseveres (because she believes God will never leave her and will give her the strength to make wise choices and stick with them). _____ never fails (because her value and worthiness of love are not contingent on what she does but on what God says about her. Regardless of what happens in her life, she believes God loves her and will never fail her).

How did you do? After reading the passage with your name inserted, can you honestly say you are loving yourself the way God does? Are you extending His love for you toward yourself? It won't get any easier by putting it off. You won't just wake up one day and say, "You know what, Self? I'm going to love you someday the way God does!" Just as you get to make the conscious decision to receive God's love for you, you also get to make the conscious decision to love yourself as He does. Loving yourself in this way won't happen overnight, but it will grow with time as you practice it.

Still today, when I catch myself using the litmus test of perfectionism instead of the litmus test of God's love for me, I have to pause and remind myself that I am lovable. I am valuable. I am these things because God loves me with no strings attached. Clip the strings today. Those strings will serve as a noose around your neck if you let them. Don't let them. Instead, choose to love yourself as God does.

Do you know what the cool outcome is of receiving God's love for you? You begin to fall in love with Him. Remember when I shared that you can't give away what you don't have? When you choose to receive His love for you, then you have it to give away. First, back to Him, then to yourself, and then to others in a whole new way. This love is not based on conditions but on who He is and who He says you are to Him. Once you understand that you are loved simply for the love of it and not for what you do or don't do, a whole new world opens for you. You are no longer bound by performance. You are free to be who you were created to be.

When this really sank in for me, I knew my life and the way I related to people were going to take on a whole new meaning. Once I realized I am fully loved and fully accepted just as I am by God, I was able to learn to love others in this way. When I catch myself slipping into old ways of thinking, I remind myself that it's not about what I can do or what others can do for me. Rather, it is about simply loving God and receiving His love, so I can love others the way He loves me. When others disappoint us, and they will, it is a game changer when we can tell ourselves, "It's okay. They're trying to figure out this thing called life too. We're all at different places. It's okay when people don't understand me. God does and always will."

So it all begins and ends with love. Once you begin applying this kind of love to yourself, then you can love others with no strings attached.

I want to reiterate a very important truth. I have said this in different ways throughout this book, but when I was where you are, I needed to hear it many times before it finally stuck. When abuse is present, you cannot love your abuser into wellness. While I will always have a love for Ben, I finally accepted that loving him would not change him. As a survivor of abuse, the healthy choice is to love your abuser from a distance and to love yourself enough to let go. Not all survivors will still have a love for their abusers, and that's perfectly understandable. But for those of us who do, we need to accept this very important truth: no amount of our love will change our partners, regardless of how long or how hard we try. It's only in accepting God's love for us, and accepting the limits of our love to change another person, that true healing can take place.

Leave Him Loving Him

When I was working in a domestic violence shelter many years ago, a young mother of four came to our shelter seeking support and a place to live for her and her kids. I was working a double shift one night. After she put her little ones to bed, she and I stayed up folding clothes in the donation room. She shared with me her story, and at the end she said, "When I told my abusive husband I was going to leave him, I told him I was going to leave him, loving him."

That's the part many people don't get. We loved these men. We thought they loved us. In their own twisted way, some believe they did. The point is, loving yourself with the same kind of love God loves you with is a must to healing well. I can't say it enough. You will never be all God created you to be until you love yourself like He does. It's a process. I understand this. But, it is a process that can't be skipped, minimized or detoured around. The only way out is through.

Through His love.

We Attract Where We're At

Let's take a moment to remind ourselves of a highly important truth. Abusers don't come holding a sign that reads:

I'm really a jerk. After I've charmed you enough that I know I've got you, I'm going to do a 180 on you, making your life hell. You'll be so confused, and your life will be so upside down that you'll deny your reality and do all you can to fix me. I'll make you feel it's impossible to leave me, and if you try, I'll crank up the crazy, leaving you emotionally, physically, and, if I can pull it off, financially busted.

If they came with a sign like that, you would run for the hills. Unfortunately, they carry no sign issuing a warning of imminent harm. Many women miss or minimize early warning signs that an abuser may exhibit while they are dating. The onset of abuse often creates a lot of anxiety and confusion because many abusers can be very charming. The confusion comes when the charmer turns aggressive verbally, physically, and/or psychologically. Appendix Q describes some of these early signs. Being aware of these can help you see, leave, or avoid an unhealthy relationship in the future.

At the same time, I have observed a very interesting phenomenon over the years. I have also recognized it in myself. We do attract where we're at. When I first met the man who would later become my abusive partner, I was naïve, masked insecurity like a pro, performance driven, and super hungry for love and attention—especially from a male. Although I have a very deep love for my father, I always wanted to feel closer to him when I was growing up. He worked constantly and placed immense pressure on me to perform well and be successful. Because I never felt truly known by him, I yearned to be known by someone, specifically a male someone. You know the rest of the story.

I can't overemphasize how massively important it is for you to remain honest with yourself and to remind yourself that this journey doesn't have a final depot where you exit the train. The healing well journey continues throughout your entire life. Why? Because as long as you're alive, you have the opportunity to grow and learn. If you stop growing and learning, you stop living and instead are merely existing.

The moment you committed to healing well, your life started down a new track. By shifting your trajectory from victim to survivor to overcomer, you and your relationship choices, along with their consequences, are changing for the better.

My prayer is that you stay the course and that your unique path leads you to whatever your heart's desires may be. Not everyone wants to be in another intimate relationship with a life partner. That's perfectly fine. What matters is that you acquire all life can be for you, personally, regardless of what that entails. Everything I have shared with you about healthy love applies to all relationships, both platonic and intimate. You will discover, if you haven't already, that your friendships will be healthier as you become healthier. The principle remains—you attract where you're at.

But if you do decide to pursue an intimate relationship, you need to know you can stand alone before you stand with someone else. As a matter of fact, serial relationships are often an indication a person is insecure about being alone. They use one relationship to try to heal from another, or they simply are uncomfortable not having an intimate partner. The emotional injury an abusive relationship causes requires that you allow ample time to intentionally pursue healing well before you get into another relationship.

Since we attract where we're at, you will begin to see that as you become emotionally healthier, you will draw emotionally healthy people to you. My motto has become "Don't marry your ministry!" meaning, do not get into an intimate relationship with a project, with someone who is not emotionally healthy or is going to abuse you. A healthy intimate relationship is one that energizes you, encourages you to grow, and results in you feeling more alive.

When you are ready to consider a future intimate relationship, the litmus test of 1 Corinthians 13 still applies. When you're embarking on a new relationship, place his name where the word *love* appears in the passage to see if healthy and true love is budding between the two of you.

For example, if you are noticing jealousy rather than kindness or angry outbursts rather than patience, that person is not loving you in the true manner we are to love one another. Once the novelty of a new relationship begins to wane, you will be able to see what's real and what was simply for show. Pay attention to what you see and sense. Please do not minimize it. Use the description of love in 1 Corinthians 13 as a gauge and a source of protection from future harm. As you learn to love yourself in this manner, it will also be the standard by which you can determine if someone truly loves you.

Learning What "Normal" Looks Like

When I knew I was ready to begin dating, I was scared out of my wits! I wish I could read the bubble above your head right now, many of you may be thinking, "Are you serious? This woman goes through all of this healing well stuff and she's still scared?" Yep, I was. Actually, borderline petrified is a better fit for how I felt, at least initially.

Remember, I grew up pretty isolated. Went to an all-girls school for a chunk of my education. Married after my first year of college. Was married for almost two decades. Didn't date while our six-year divorce laboriously stagnated in family court. After the divorce, I "pseudo dated" someone from my past, which allowed me to hide out in my comfort zone of the familiar.

About that time, my brother—the one who had asked me years earlier where my moxie had gone—called me on the carpet once again. He's great at that. He told me I had to stop hiding. Dating again wasn't something I had to fear. He told me I needed to let go of my past entirely, meaning any hold my prior spouse still had on me. I had to be the one to let go and move forward. In numerous ways, I had already done that. But when it came to the thought of dating again, a part of me wanted to hold on to whatever tiny morsels of "stuckness" that still remained. I'm not sure why, but my brother's confidence in me gave me the confidence I needed to step out into the dating world again. He encouraged me to consider online dating, specifically eHarmony.

Was he crazy? I didn't need eHarmony! Didn't he know I was going to meet my future beau in the frozen food aisle of the grocery store at 11:00 p.m.? The truth was the only people I "met" in the grocery store at 11:00 p.m. were clerks, shelf stockers, and other people buying their midnight snack of chocolate peanut butter ice cream like I was! Just as my brother was right about my moxie, he was also absolutely right about me stepping out and trying something new, even if it was uncomfortable and unfamiliar.

Certainly, people can and do meet in random places every day, but that's not what was happening for me. Since my brother had met his precious wife through eHarmony, I thought I'd give it a shot. If nothing else, I was going to get him off my back along with the rest of my family and friends who were also a part of his online dating posse!

After a few weeks rolled by, I asked two of my young adult kids to sit with me at Starbucks while I filled out my online dating profile. They graciously agreed. As I bounced my answers off them, they gave me a thumbs-up or a "Mom, that's definitely not you!" roll of the eyes, letting me know if my responses were truly reflective of me. I also had Chelsey review my profile. I spent a couple weeks completing the questionnaire because I wanted it to be a true representation of who I was. And I didn't include just pictures in which my makeup and hair were done. I shared pictures of me with no makeup, pictures of me with my kids, and others that portrayed me as I really am. Not perfect. But real. After I launched my profile, I waited. The matches started to pop up in my inbox. But I still wanted to pace myself and pray through this process.

One morning I spent time reading the story of Joseph in the Bible. If you're not familiar with this story, I encourage you to read it. It starts in Genesis 37 and ends in Genesis 50. What you will see is that Joseph went through many tough trials in his life. He had moments when things were great and times that were beyond bad.

As I sat there thinking about this Joseph guy, it occurred to me that through all his various trials, he maintained his integrity and his faith. His character was stellar. He was a wise business-man. He loved his family. He was a good friend. Then it hit me! I wanted a Joseph! I remember it like it was yesterday. I literally shot straight up in bed and said it out loud, as if Jesus Himself was sitting right there next to me. "Jesus, I want a Joseph!" I wanted someone I could truly trust with my heart. Someone who respected me, respected himself, and was respected by others. Someone who wasn't going to abuse me, neglect me, or leave me. I wanted a true gentleman who loved God, loved himself, and would love me as I deserved. I was now ready to "treat myself to normal."

I grabbed a blank sheet of paper and started listing the quali-ties and the attributes I wanted to further develop in myself as someone's future wife. I then wrote what I desired in my future husband. It may sound corny, but writing it all out actually helped me to clearly sort through my honest desires. The list was long. But I didn't care. I wanted to write down every single thing, even my desire that my husband would have hair! I'm not kidding. I included a full head of hair. Why not? The Bible says, "You do not have because you do not ask God" (James 4:2). I was asking without restraint. I was ready to meet my Joseph.

As I filtered through my eHarmony responses, I quickly realized this was not some sort of a cyberspace magic wand. Chelsey and I spent many hours looking at my potential matches, vacillating between laughing hysterically and being utterly shocked by some of the responses. I'll never forget one in particular we nicknamed "Catman" because all of his profile pictures were of his cats! Cats in hats. Cats in ties. Cats performing acrobatics. I wish I was jok-ing here, but I'm not! In one of the feline photos, Catman told the lucky lady that if she could guess what his cat was thinking then she got a "free coke."

Are you serious? I am. You can't make this kind of stuff up!

If you're going to entertain the option of online dating, it is by no means a straight shot from Cupid's arrow to your heart. It takes time, patience, a good sense of humor, and—what I believe helped me the most—an honest profile of yourself. Not all fluffed up, but honest.

Never one to easily give up, despite the oddity of Catman, I continued on my quest. Finally, I came upon a match that caught my eye. You see, at the very bottom of my profile I had written an important comment. I said, "If you've ever abused or cheated on your wife or girlfriend, please don't contact me." The reason his response got my attention was because he was the only one who bothered to acknowledge my important request. His response was, "Regarding your final comment, I have done neither, nor will I ever." On our first date, I asked him, "Why did you respond to my comment about abuse and cheating? No one else did." He replied, "If it was important enough for you to include it, it was important I respond to it." I immediately sensed his sincerity. I would quickly discover that his integrity and character were not an act. A true gentleman exudes both. I had found a true gentleman. A Joseph.

Dating again taught me a lot about myself too. I realized I really had learned to trust my gut again. While some matches were easy to weed out, others needed more consideration. I combed through many suggested matches and communicated with the men who seemed plausible and honest.

It was my mother's wise counsel that really helped me. She said in her candid sort of way, "Enjoy yourself, Ramona. Relax. Just throw your head back and laugh." That was good advice. I needed to simply enjoy meeting new people and not take myself so seriously. I appreciated her advice so much that I had a personalized license plate made for my car that read, "LGHALOT." I was done with crying. It was finally time for me to laugh again.

That's precisely one of the things I noticed when I first met my future husband. We laughed a lot together. I recall early in our dating, laughing so hard with him that I had tears running down my face! I enjoyed being with him. I felt truly relaxed. I could be myself with no pressure to be anything or anyone else. I felt fully accepted. He gave me all the space and time I needed to move forward in our relationship with no expectations or control. I felt a new sort of freedom I had never experienced before. His emotional maturity was very attractive to me. I could tell early on that the super-traits I had relied on so heavily in my previous relationship would not be taken advantage of in this one. He was confident but not arrogant. He was truly kind with a gentle spirit that even my family and friends quickly discerned was genuine.

About a year and a half later, while goofing around in the kitchen, he randomly said to me, in the worst Italian accent I've ever heard, "Just call me Giuseppe!" My jaw hit the ground. Did I hear him right? Did he just say to call him Giuseppe? Giuseppe is Italian for Joseph. He was right. He was and always will be my Giuseppe. Shortly thereafter, we wed encircled by our beautiful children, who had lovingly and patiently supported both of us through some very long and painful years. On that gorgeous fall day, I read from the list I had penned several years prior. My list had become my vows.

I desired what I referred to as a Joseph. Your desires may be different than mine, and that's perfectly fine. What I'm encouraging you to do is really think through your true, heartfelt desires and not settle for less. As you continue growing into your strongest self, determine that your future partner will be someone who also recognizes the value of healing well from his own hurts and disappointments, that he too has worked on himself and, like you, prioritizes continuing to grow.

Ready to Love, *Really* Love Again

As I type this chapter, my Sweetie is sitting at his desk working nearby. I can hear him talking to himself out loud as if I wasn't in the room. I love this about him. I cherish this about us. There is a comfortableness in each other's presence that is like a coming home sort of feeling and slipping into your favorite pair of old slippers. It's wonderful! I never imagined this or should I say, I never imagined *he* was around the bend in my life!

When I say, "around the bend," keep in mind it wasn't a quick jaunt. I spent many years working on myself and staying connected with emotionally healthy people who supported me. Counseling is work. Healing well is no walk in the park. It's tough to look at yourself, and it can be equally as tough accepting "what is" regarding your relationship. The alternative, however, will cost you dearly. Denial always does.

Reflecting back, if I could do it all over again, the only part I'd change is the pain my kids went through. That I'd erase with a big, giant eraser if I could. But for me, I am grateful for who I've become. The process of healing well, so today I can live free, was worth all the effort. I truly believe every tear had a purpose and brought me to where I am now. Today I am an overcomer by God's grace, His unconditional love, and my commitment to learning, growing, and healing. Every morning I now wake up to coffee brewing, a warm hug, and someone who tells me he adores me.

So to circle back to the beginning, how did I get from being shaken like a rag doll, wearing sunglasses indoors to conceal a black eye, consistently being called horrific names to now experiencing healthy love in the context of a safe, tender, and passionate relationship? I stayed the course. I stayed committed to the healing journey. I stayed committed to myself.

I never quit. And, I firmly believe you have this same resolve too.

You haven't done all this work on and in yourself to lower your bar now. Appendix R provides a comparative guide describing healthy versus unhealthy relationships. Having clear standards for yourself and for the person you may choose to partner with is healthy and wise. You know so much more than you once did.

Continue utilizing this valuable information, especially when it comes to a potential future partner. And remember to stay connected with your "citadel" as you go through the dating process. They can help you see possible red flags or if something doesn't seem quite right.

It's Your Turn Now

So that's my story. You began telling your story at the start of this book. You're not done yet. Your story can have a happy ending. You have the tools and you have the will. Most importantly, you have a heavenly Father looking out for you, guiding you with His unfailing love. Don't ever give up on God. He hears you. He sees you. He loves you. You have cried long enough. It's time now for you to really enjoy your life and throw your head back and laugh!

Heal well. Live free. Dream big.

I believe in you. I have believed for you.

Now . . . go believe in yourself!

Questions to Ponder

1. As you reflect on the phrase "free to love, *really* love again," what thoughts come to your mind as this pertains to you? What feelings does this stir inside you?

2. How has your experience in an abusive relationship affected your desire to meet someone new?

3. How is your commitment to healing well preparing you for the possibility of a future relationship?

4. Are there areas in which you believe you still need to grow and heal before you fully open your heart and life to a new person? What are those areas?

5. After reading what emotionally healthy love looks like, do you believe you are loving yourself in this manner? Where do you shine? Where do you falter?

6. Have you made the committed decision to have an intimate relationship only with someone who loves you in the 1 Corinthians 13 sort of way? Remember to refer back to this litmus test for love as your gauge for a healthy relationship.

7. You have learned a great deal, and you have come a long way. How has your belief level in yourself changed? How have your beliefs about God's love and His heart for you been affected? How have these new acquired beliefs affected how you view yourself?

8. Take a moment to write how you intend to remain committed to healing well and living free for the rest of your life. Reflect on this when you feel weary or discouraged. Share it with a trusted friend who can come alongside you when you need a gentle reminder of how far you've come.

Prayer of Reflection

Jesus, I was so broken and carrying such deep pain inside that I never thought it was possible to experience the budding freedom and genuine healing that are growing in my life today. You saw me when I lost sight of myself. You saw a future for me I never imagined. I still have moments when I struggle with doubt and fear. But I know You are with me. I know You understand me. I know You do not hold my frailty against me. Thank You, Jesus, that when I am weak, through You I am strong (2 Corinthians 12:9–10). I ask You to heal any remaining places within me that keep me from being all You created me to be. Please replace any residual effects from the abuse with strength and an authentic love for myself. I ask You to do the same for my children. Heal them where they still hurt and struggle. Only You can bring good out of this pain for me and for my kids.

Help me to never permit anyone to abuse me or treat me in any way that does not reflect true love, the kind of love in 1 Corinthians 13. Mold me into that kind of lover. I want to love You, myself, and others as You love me. Apart from You, this is impossible. Hold me close by Your side. If I ever start to wander, come get me and bring me back into Your fold. Thank You for being the conduit through which healing well and living free have translated into my life. Please continue to lead my steps, my choices, and my life as You know best. I surrender myself into Your hands, the safest place for me to be. I love You. Thank You for loving me first. Amen.

God's Enduring Promises

We love because he first loved us. (1 John 4:19)

It is for freedom that Christ has set us free. Stand firm, then, and do not let yourselves be burdened again by a yoke of slavery. (Galatians 5:1)

> Trust in the LORD and do good.
>   Then you will live safely in the land and prosper.
> Take delight in the LORD,
>   and he will give you your heart's desires.
> Commit everything you do to the LORD.
>   Trust him, and he will help you. (Psalm 37:3–5 NLT)

> Wait patiently for the LORD.
>   Be brave and courageous.
>   Yes, wait patiently for the LORD. (Psalm 27:14 NLT)

Have I not commanded you? Be strong and of good courage; do not be afraid, nor be dismayed, for the LORD your God *is* with you wherever you go. (Joshua 1:9 NKJV)

And I am certain that God, who began the good work within you, will continue his work until it is finally finished on the day when Christ Jesus returns. (Philippians 1:6 NLT)

My Promise and Prayer for You

As I bring this book to a close, I'd like to leave you with a promise and a prayer. My promise is that you will remain in my prayers for the rest of my life. To me, prayer is both a privilege and a responsibility. Although our lives have not physically intersected, our stories have. Stories that involve pain, regardless of the unique nuisances, bind people together in a way few things can. Thank you for entrusting me to walk alongside you as you have embarked on the most courageous journey ever: facing your pain with courage and determination so you can authentically heal and experience what it means to be truly free on the deepest level. My first prayer for you is below. Together, my Sweetie and I will continue to bring you and your needs before the throne of Jesus. Know with confidence you are being prayed for. And we know that when we pray, He hears us. That's His promise!

Sweet Jesus, with all my heart I want to thank You for coming alongside my friend and me as together we have traversed the healing well journey laid out in the pages of this book. You alone are fully aware of their pain and the details of their story. You alone are fully aware of the deep, miry pit that they were in. Only You can reach down into their abyss and draw them out. Thank You for the promise that Your hand is never too short to save. You are able to reach us regardless of how deep our pit is or how excruciating our pain may be.

Please allow them to feel You especially when they doubt You most. Meet them wherever they are and continue to hold their hand in the days ahead.

I may never meet them, but we share a bond that only those who have walked this path truly understand. I know and trust that You will continue to walk beside them, hold them, and remind them that You will never leave them. When they stumble, as we all do, lift them up, dust them off, and put the skip back into their step so they can continue moving forward with You. Open their eyes and heart to see and know You as You truly are. Wherever faulty thinking about themselves, You, or their future remains, please heal those areas and replace misunderstanding with Your truth. Help them to see that their pain will not be wasted. Rather, their pain will be used for good in ways they may not recognize now.

Help them to trust You, to believe in You, and to allow You to love them as You so earnestly desire. In turn, help them to love themselves as You love them. Unconditionally. Keep Your hand of protection upon them. Grant them the desires of their heart. Daily whisper to them, "It is for freedom that I have set you free." Give them the wisdom to walk in this freedom and to treasure it as a gift directly from Your hand to theirs. In Your beautiful name, Jesus, I pray. Amen.

A Personal Word to You

If you have never made the decision to commit your life and heart to Jesus, I encourage you to not let this moment slip away. A personal relationship with Jesus Christ is not about do's and don'ts. It's not about religion or rituals. It's about relationship. We don't have to get all cleaned up to embrace His love and forgiveness.

He took care of "cleaning us all up" when He went to the cross. His death and resurrection is the reason we can be forgiven and set free. He paid the price for our sin. Something we could never do for ourselves. Something we can only choose to receive as the gift it was intended to be. You are unconditionally loved by God. His Son's nail-pierced hands and feet testify to His love for you. Will you open your heart to Jesus and let Him in? If so, pray with me now . . .

> *Jesus, I have come a long way and done a tremendous amount of work to get here. I have had conversations with You all throughout this book. However, I know I have never made the conscious decision to ask You into my life. Today, Jesus, I ask you to forgive me of my sins. I ask you to wash me clean through Your shed blood on the cross. I ask You to be my Lord and Savior from this day forward. I don't want to live another day apart from You. Thank You, Jesus, for wrapping me in Your arms and holding me forevermore. Amen.*

If you prayed this prayer (or something similar in your own words) know your name has been permanently written on the palm of His hand (Isaiah 49:16). This is a huge cause to celebrate! I encourage you to connect with a healthy church community. One that loves Jesus and loves people. Your decision today will not magically make life a stroll in the park, but it will give you the assurance that you are never alone. Jesus will continue to walk with you through the ups and downs of your life, giving you comfort when you are weary and celebrating over you when life is great. Today you made the most important decision you could ever make! I'm so happy for you I could turn cartwheels!!

Healing Well and Living Free: A Guide for Overcomers

I want you to have a quick reference you can flip to whenever you need a reminder of where you were and how far you've come. Below are two lists. One describes a victim's mind-set and responses to intimate partner violence, and the other describes an overcomer's new way of thinking and responding. Remember, healing well is a process that will not be accomplished overnight. Remind yourself that you're moving forward because you are intentionally choosing what overcomers do in order to heal well and live free. As you continue your journey, you will see how each of the descriptors below comes to fruition in your life. Stay the course. Remember my words: "You're worth it!"

VICTIM Instead of . . .	OVERCOMER You're now committed to . . .
• staying silent	• no longer hiding, seeking wise counsel, and sharing your story
• remaining in isolation	• connecting with a healthy community
• having poor boundaries	• setting healthy boundaries that are consistently enforced
• minimizing abuse	• seeing abuse for what it is

VICTIM *Instead of . . .*	OVERCOMER *You're now committed to . . .*
• rationalizing abuse	• calling abuse what it is
• lowering the bar by permitting yourself to be treated with disrespect, disregard, and disdain	• setting a new bar that encompasses being treated consistently with healthy love, respect, and value
• tolerating abuse	• separating yourself from your abuser
• trying to fix your abuser	• redirecting your energy toward working on yourself
• minimizing or ignoring red flags	• recognizing and responding to red flags and believing them when you see them
• being unaware of the cycle of abuse	• recognizing the cyclical pattern, knowing it will continue to repeat itself and get worse over time, and extracting yourself from this pattern
• losing contact with family and friends	• reestablishing connections with emotionally healthy family members and friends
• believing abuse is a couple's issue, a communication problem, or an inability to resolve conflict	• placing the responsibility for abusive behavior solely on your abuser, knowing you didn't cause it and can't cure it, and realizing that healthy conflict never results in abuse
• praying more, believing more, and trying harder with the faulty belief that your abuser will change as a result	• praying for your personal healing and growth, trusting that good will result from the pain you've experienced, and accepting that you cannot love someone into wellness
• defending your abuser and making excuses for him	• admitting the truth about your abuser's abusive behavior and no longer covering up for him
• ignoring the effects abuse has had on you	• seeking professional help for PTSD, depression, anxiety, or any other conditions resulting from trauma

VICTIM	OVERCOMER
Instead of . . .	*You're now committed to . . .*
• living with faulty perceptions of God	• getting honest with God, opening your heart to discovering His true nature, and accepting that God loves you unconditionally
• feeling shame	• differentiating between what you do and who you are
• harboring unforgiveness toward your abuser, those who have not believed your story or have minimized your pain, and yourself	• remaining open to learning the true meaning of healthy forgiveness, making the decision to apply it by faith, and understanding that forgiveness does not require reconciliation
• ignoring your gut	• trusting your gut
• wearing masks—pretending	• striving for congruency between your public self and your private self
• ignoring your grief	• permitting yourself to grieve by feeling and expressing your emotions
• displacing or stuffing your anger	• identifying and expressing your anger in a healthy way
• placing higher value on the marriage than on your safety and well-being	• possessing an accurate understanding regarding the value of marriage versus the value of human life and giving your safety and well-being precedence over maintaining the marriage
• adhering to faulty biblical interpretations surrounding domestic violence, marital covenant, and divorce	• obtaining an accurate understanding of what the Bible teaches regarding how domestic violence severs the marriage covenant
• using substances (drugs, alcohol, food) to numb yourself	• finding freedom from addiction
• diminishing self-care	• intentionally valuing yourself by taking quality care of yourself physically, emotionally, etc.

VICTIM *Instead of . . .*	OVERCOMER *You're now committed to . . .*
• downplaying symptoms such as headaches, digestive complaints, autoimmune responses, and night terrors	• understanding that your body is sending you signals that you are no longer willing to ignore
• trusting people too soon	• extending trust only to those who have earned it and have demonstrated they are trustworthy
• self-sabotaging by having an unhealthy love toward yourself	• growing in your understanding of healthy love and applying it to yourself
• trying to appear perfect	• being who you really are and no longer a people pleaser
• masking insecurities	• accepting who you are and no longer comparing yourself to others
• allowing fear to control and manipulate you	• no longer being governed by fear or allowing people to manipulate you, instead being led by peace and trusting God
• ignoring concerns expressed by friends and family members	• listening to and valuing concerns expressed by friends and family members
• being codependent, over-responsible, or over-functioning	• allowing others to do for themselves what they're capable of doing and no longer making excuses for irresponsible behavior
• being confused and doubting yourself	• adhering to your convictions and no longer struggling with self-doubt
• losing sight of personal dreams and goals and forgetting what makes you feel alive	• intentionally pursuing your dreams and goals, being future-focused, and pursuing your destiny
• withering away on the inside and perhaps even on the outside	• choosing to live, *really* live again
• fearing that you will never intimately love again	• embracing the option to love, *really* love again

Appendix A

Abuse Evaluation Form

Directions: Circle the words or phrases that describe what you have experienced in your relationship, even if it happened only once.

Physical Abuse

The misuse of size, strength, or presence to control or hurt someone.

- Pushing
- Shoving
- Backhanding
- Biting
- Strangling
- Punching
- Burning
- Hair pulling
- Kneeling
- Smothering

- Grabbing
- Kicking
- Stabbing or cutting with a knife
- Smacking repeatedly or a single slap leaving a mark
- Throwing objects
- Breaking furniture
- Sweeping objects off a table or dresser
- Breaking a windshield or windows
- Intentionally breaking your personal items
- Punching or kicking a wall or door
- Clenching a fist as if to hit
- Twisting your arms
- Tearing your clothes
- Standing or sitting on you
- Banging your head or pinning you against a wall or the floor
- Holding or carrying you against your will
- Trying to hit you with a car or pushing you out of a car
- Driving recklessly in order to scare you
- Blocking a doorway so you can't leave
- Standing behind your car so you can't drive away
- Taking your keys so you can't drive away
- Disabling your phone to prevent a call
- Locking you in or out of the house, in a closet, or in another confined space
- Abusing or killing a pet

Verbal/Emotional Abuse

The misuse of words or voice to control or hurt someone.

- Yelling
- Humiliating

- Name-calling
- Laughing at or making fun of
- Manipulating
- Lying
- Discounting
- Blackmailing
- Threatening to abuse, divorce, report to welfare, kill, or commit suicide
- Threatening to hurt the kids, to take them away, or to keep them from your family
- Accusing you of infidelity
- Having affairs
- Checking up on you, following you, or stalking you
- Controlling who you see or talk to or what you read
- Making you drop legitimate charges
- Limiting outside involvement
- Questioning paternity
- Using insults/put-downs of you or your friends
- Criticizing your appearance
- Preventing you from attending school or work
- Minimizing your concerns
- Saying you caused the abusive behavior
- Using jealousy to justify abusive actions
- Acting withdrawn and silent
- Displaying or brandishing weapons
- Coercing you to do something illegal
- Making you feel guilty about the children, mistakes, house-keeping, etc.
- Making you feel afraid; intimidating with looks, actions, or gestures

- Playing mind games
- Denying that the abuse happened
- Treating you like a servant
- Being the only one to define roles in the relationship

Spiritual Abuse (a form of Emotional Abuse)

The misuse and misapplication of religious values or teachings to control or hurt someone.

- Enforcing control-oriented leadership; in effect, lording it over you
- Demanding you to be submissive with unquestioning loyalty and obedience
- Not allowing you to question him or his decisions
- Using guilt, fear, intimidation, and verses out of context to control you
- Claiming that questioning him is akin to questioning God

Financial Abuse

The misuse of knowledge, position, and relationship to take advantage of someone financially.

- Restricting your access to family funds
- Keeping detailed track of your money use
- Making you ask for money
- Grilling you for information about activities and money use
- Taking away money, checkbook, credit cards, or bank cards
- Wasting family money on drugs or alcohol
- Refusing to keep a job or to let you work
- Participating in asset fraud

- Lying about how much money he has or does not have
- Not letting you know about family income
- Giving you an allowance
- Gambling with family funds

Sexual Abuse

A sexual act committed against someone without that person's freely given consent. Luring, tricking, trapping, coercing, or bribing anyone with less maturity or power into a sexual experience.

- Sexually stimulating or being stimulated by anyone disempowered by age, size, handicap, or situation (This stimulation could be physical, verbal, or visual, including discussing or describing, watching, revealing, or fondling.)
- Derogatory name-calling
- Deliberately causing unwanted physical pain during sex
- Deliberately passing on sexual diseases or infections
- Using objects, toys, or other items without your consent and to cause pain or humiliation
- Using pornography in any form
- Forcing participation in acting out fantasies or scenes from pornography
- Insisting that you watch pornography
- Refusing to use condoms or to allow you to use other forms of birth control
- Forcing an abortion
- Forcing sex, even within marriage
- Forcing sex with others
- Forcing oral or anal sex
- Indecent exposure

- Repeatedly withholding sex within marriage
- Pouting if reasonably declined sex
- Hitting while you are pregnant
- Rape
- Incest

Appendix B

Safety Plans

Preparing to Leave Safety Plan

Because violence could escalate when a victim tries to leave, here are some things to keep in mind before you prepare to take that step:

- Keep any evidence of physical abuse, such as pictures of injuries.
- Keep a journal of all violent incidences, noting dates, events, and threats made, if possible. Keep your journal in a safe place.
- Know where you can go to get help. Tell someone what is happening to you.
- If you are injured, go to a doctor or an emergency room and report what happened to you. Ask that they document your visit.
- Plan with your children and identify a safe place for them to go, such as a room with a lock or a friend's house where they can go for help. Reassure them that their job is to stay safe, not to protect you.

- Contact your local shelter and find out about laws and other resources available to you before you have to use them during a crisis. WomensLaw.org has state-by-state legal information.
- Acquire job skills or take courses at a community college as you can.
- Try to set aside money or ask friends or family members to hold money for you.

When You Are Leaving Safety Plan

Make a plan for how and where you will escape quickly. You may request a police escort when you leave. Use the following list of items as a guide for what you need to bring with you. You can also call 800-799-SAFE (7233) to speak with an advocate who can help you come up with a personalized safety plan for leaving.

1. Identification
   - Driver's license
   - Birth certificates for you and your children
   - Social security cards

2. Legal Papers
   - Protective order
   - Copies of any lease or rental agreements or the deed to your home
   - Car registration and insurance papers
   - Health and life insurance papers
   - Medical records for you and your children
   - School records
   - Work permit/green card/visa
   - Passport

- Divorce and custody papers
- Marriage license

3. Emergency Numbers
   - Your local police and/or sheriff's department
   - Your local domestic violence program or shelter
   - Friends, relatives, and family members
   - Your local doctor's office and hospital
   - County and/or district attorney's office

4. Other
   - Money and/or credit cards (in your name)
   - Checking and/or savings account books
   - Financial information
   - Medications
   - Extra set of house and car keys
   - Valuable jewelry
   - Pay-as-you-go cell phone
   - Address book
   - Pictures and sentimental items
   - Several changes of clothes for you and your children

After You Have Left Safety Plan

You should have a safety plan to ensure your continued safety after you have left an abusive relationship. Here are some safety precautions to consider:

- Change your locks and phone number.
- Call the telephone company to request caller ID. Ask that your phone number be blocked so that if you call anyone,

neither your partner nor anyone else will be able to get your new, unlisted phone number.

- Change your work hours and the route you take to work.
- Change the route you take to transport your children to school or consider changing your children's schools.
- Alert school authorities of the situation.
- If you have a restraining order, keep a certified copy of it with you at all times. Call law enforcement to enforce the restraining order and give copies of the order to friends, employers, neighbors, and schools, along with a picture of the offender.
- Consider renting a post office box or using the address of a friend for your mail (be aware that addresses are on restraining orders and police reports, and be careful to whom you give your new address and phone number).
- Reschedule appointments that the offender is aware of.
- Use different stores and frequent different social spots.
- Alert neighbors and request that they call the police if they feel you may be in danger.
- Replace wooden doors with steel or metal doors. Install security systems if possible.
- Install a motion sensitive lighting system.
- Tell people you work with about the situation and have your calls screened by a receptionist if possible.
- Explain your situation to people who take care of your children or drive them/pick them up from school and activities. Provide them with a copy of the restraining order.

The above material was adapted from the National Center for Victims of Crime, "What Is a Safety Plan?" The National Domestic Violence Hotline, 1998, http://www.thehotline.org/help/path-to-safety/.

Appendix C

Hotlines and Resources

National Domestic Violence Resources

- **National Domestic Violence Hotline**: 800-799-SAFE (7233) or 800-787-3224 (TTY); www.TheHotline.org—This is a crisis intervention and referral phone line for domestic violence.

- **Resource Center on Domestic Violence: Child Protection and Custody**: 800-527-3223; www.rcdvcpc.org/—This resource provides information and resources on these important topics to judges, domestic violence advocates, and the public.

- **National Coalition Against Domestic Violence**: 303-839-8459 or 303-839-1852 (TTY); www.ncadv.org—The mission of the National Coalition Against Domestic Violence is to organize for collective power by advancing transformative work, thinking, and leadership of communities and individuals working to end the violence.

- **National Center for Victims of Crime**: 202-467-8700; www
  .ncvc.org—The mission of the National Center for Victims of Crime is to forge a national commitment to help victims of crime rebuild their lives. The center is dedicated to serving individuals, families, and communities harmed by crime.

- **National Organization for Victim Assistance**: 800-TRY-NOVA (879-6682); www.TryNOVA.org—This organization is composed of victim and witness assistance programs and practitioners, criminal justice agencies and professionals, mental health professionals, researchers, former victims and survivors, and others committed to the recognition and implementation of victim rights and services.

- **National Online Resource Center on Violence Against Women**: www.VAWnet.org—The mission of VAWnet is to harness and use electronic communication technology to end violence against women.

- **National Resource Center on Domestic Violence**: 800-537-2238 or 800-553-2508 (TTY); www.nrcdv.org—This organization makes information available to those who want to help by educating themselves on the issues facing victims of domestic violence.

- **National Sexual Violence Resource Center**: 877-739-3895 or 717-909-0715 (TTY); www.nsvrc.org—This resource identifies, develops, and disseminates resources regarding all aspects of sexual violence prevention and intervention.

- **Domestic Violence Awareness Handbook**: www.dm.usda .gov/shmd/handbook.htm—This guide to domestic violence covers common myths, what to say to a victim, and what communities can do about the problem.

State Domestic Violence Resource

- **Domestic Shelters**: www.DomesticShelters.org—This website provides information on domestic violence help and local shelters. It also includes a directory of state offices that can help victims find local support, shelter, and free or low-cost legal services. Includes all US states as well as the District of Columbia, Puerto Rico, and the Virgin Islands.

Rape and Sexual Violence Resource

- **Rape, Abuse & Incest National Network**: 800-656-HOPE (4673); www.rainn.org—This "is the nation's largest anti-sexual violence organization. RAINN created and operates the National Sexual Assault Hotline . . . in partnership with more than 1,000 local sexual assault service providers across the country and operates the DoD Safe Helpline for the Department of Defense. RAINN also carries out programs to prevent sexual violence, help survivors, and ensure that perpetrators are brought to justice."[1]

Resources for Parents

- **Child Welfare Information Gateway**: 800-394-3366; www .ChildWelfare.gov—This is the congressionally mandated and funded information service of the United States Children's Bureau, Administration for Children and Families, United States Department of Health and Human Services.
- **Childhelp, National Child Abuse Hotline**: 800-4-A-CHILD (800-422-4453); www.Childhelp.org—This organization provides support to the victims of child abuse through education treatment and prevention programs.

Resources for Men

- **National Domestic Violence Hotline:** 800-799-SAFE (7233) or 800-787-3224 (TTY); www.TheHotline.org—This is a crisis intervention and referral phone line for domestic violence.
- **HelpGuide.org:** www.helpguide.org/articles/abuse/help-for-abused-men.htm—This guide provides help for men who are being abused.

Resources for LGBQ/T

- **National Domestic Violence Hotline:** 800-799-SAFE (7233) or 800-787-3224 (TTY); www.TheHotline.org—This is a crisis intervention and referral phone line for domestic violence.
- **The Network/La Red:** 800-832-1901; www.tnlr.org—This is a survivor-led organization to end LGBQ/T partner abuse.

Resources for Immigrant Women

- **National Domestic Violence Hotline:** 800-799-SAFE (7233) or 800-787-3224 (TTY); www.TheHotline.org/is-this-abuse/abuse-and-immigrants/—This is a crisis intervention and referral phone line for domestic violence.
- **Department of Homeland Security:** www.dhs.gov/immigration-options-victims-crimes—US law provides several protections for legal and undocumented immigrants who have been victims of a crime. There are specific protections for victims of domestic violence, victims of certain crimes, and victims of human trafficking.

Resources for Teens

- **Alabama Coalition Against Domestic Violence**: 800-650-6522 or 800-799-7233; www.acadv.org/warning-signs/dating-violence—This guide to teen dating violence includes early warning signs that a boyfriend or girlfriend may become abusive.

Appendix D

Types of Abuse

- *Economic abuse*: puts restrictions on your employment; makes you ask for money; gives you an allowance and takes the money you earn; requires you to account for every penny you spend; spends recklessly
- *Emotional abuse*: puts you down; calls you names; plays mind games; commits mental coercion; exhibits extreme controlling behaviors; withholds affection; causes you to lose your identity
- *Financial abuse*: ruins your credit; puts cars, house, recreational equipment, and/or property in his name; spends your money; uses your credit or savings to make you dependent on him
- *Humiliation*: uses hostile humor; publicly humiliates you; criticizes you; degrades your appearance, parenting skills, housekeeping, cooking, etc.
- *Intimidation*: uses looks, actions, gestures, and voice to cause fear; argues continuously; demands that you say what he wants to hear

- *Isolation*: controls what is done, who is seen, who is talked to; limits or listens in on phone calls; sabotages car; restricts outside interests; insists on moving frequently; requires you to stay in the house; restricts access to the mail; deprives you of friends
- *Knowledge abuse*: gets therapy, goes to seminars, and uses self-help books to abuse with the knowledge he has but doesn't take responsibility for personal behaviors
- *Male privilege*: treats you like a servant; makes all the decisions; acts like "the master of the castle"
- *Medical abuse*: hurts you and does not allow you to receive medical treatment; does not allow you to receive medical treatment for normal health issues
- *Physical abuse*: abuses you by beating, biting, choking, grabbing, hitting, kicking, pinching, pulling hair, pushing, restraining, scratching, shaking, shoving, slapping, smothering, spanking, excessive tickling, tripping, twisting arms, using weapons
- *Power*: denies basic rights; uses the law to enforce his power; deprives you of a private and personal life; mandates duties; controls everything (e.g., the amount of bath water you use)
- *Property violence*: punches walls; destroys property; breaks down doors; pounds tables; abuses pets; etc.
- *Religious abuse*: uses Scripture and words such as *submission* and *obey* to abuse
- *Responsibility abuse*: makes you responsible for everything in life (e.g., bills, parenting, etc.)
- *Sexual abuse*: demands unwanted or bizarre sexual acts; physically attacks sexual parts of your body; treats you as a sex object; interrupts sleep for sex; forces sex; exhibits extreme jealousy
- *Silence*: uses silence as a weapon; does not communicate; does not express emotion

- *Stalking*: spies on you; follows you to activities (e.g., store, church, work, etc.); displays extreme distrust and jealousy
- *Threats*: threatens to end the relationship, to emotionally or physically harm you, to take the children, to commit suicide, to report you to authorities; threatens your life; forces you to break the law
- *Using children*: uses the children to give messages; uses visitation rights to harass; uses child support as leverage
- *Verbal abuse*: curses; accuses; name-calls; uses past to control and manipulate; commits mental blackmail; makes unreasonable demands

Appendix E

Cycle of Abuse

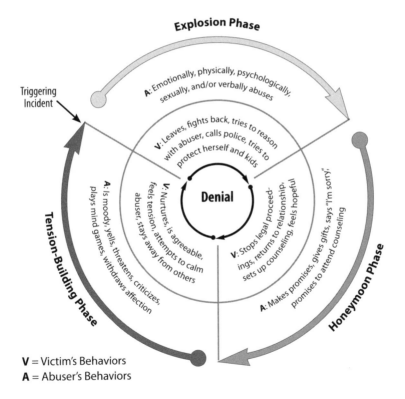

Explosion Phase

A: Emotionally, physically, psychologically, sexually, and/or verbally abuses

V: Leaves, fights back, tries to reason with abuser, calls police, tries to protect herself and kids

Triggering Incident

V: Nurtures, is agreeable, feels tension, attempts to calm abuser, stays away from others

Denial

V: Stops legal proceedings, returns to relationship, sets up counseling, feels hopeful

A: Is moody, yells, threatens criticizes, plays mind games, withdraws affection

Tension-Building Phase

A: Makes promises, gives gifts, says "I'm sorry", promises to attend counseling

Honeymoon Phase

V = Victim's Behaviors
A = Abuser's Behaviors

Below is an extended list of behaviors an abuser or a victim might display during each phase of the cycle of abuse.

	Tension-Building Phase	Explosion Phase	Honeymoon Phase
ABUSER	• Nitpicks • Is moody • Uses put-downs • Yells • Threatens • Criticizes • Plays mind games • Intimidates • Isolates victim • Destroys property • Withdraws affection • Blames victim • Embarrasses victim • Argues	• Physically abuses • Sexually abuses • Psychologically abuses • Verbally abuses • Emotionally abuses • Spiritually abuses • Uses weapon • Hits • Chokes • Humiliates • Rapes • Beats • Withholds money	• Makes promises • Sends flowers • Gives gifts • Declares love • Cries • Says "I'm sorry" • Blames others • Blames outside stress • Begs for forgiveness • Wants to make love • Says "I'll never do it again" • Enlists family support • Promises to attend counseling
VICTIM	• Nurtures • Is agreeable • Feels tension • Walks on eggshells • Tries to reason with abuser • Attempts to calm abuser • Becomes anxious • Stays away from others • Tries to appease abuser	• Leaves • Fights back • Tries to reason with abuser • Calls police • Tries to protect herself • Tries to protect the kids • Placates	• Stops legal proceedings • Returns to relationship • Sets up counseling • Agrees to stay • Feels happy • Feels hopeful

Appendix F

Reasons You May Remain in an Abusive Relationship

- You fear your abuser will become more violent, perhaps fatally so, if you try to leave.
- You want to protect your partner's and/or your family's image.
- Your partner is your support system, even though he is abusive. Psychologically, he has destroyed your outside relationships.
- You think this time will be the last time; he will change.
- You fear being a single parent with a reduced income.
- You fear he will stalk you and harass you at your workplace.
- You do not realize you have the right *not* to be abused.
- Your only desire for change is *not to be abused*.
- You fear living alone.
- You were raised in an abusive home, and this feels normal.
- You think the abuse will stop if you will only . . .

- Religious and cultural beliefs keep you in the marriage.
- You stay for the children; any father is better than none.
- Your confidence has deteriorated as a result of continuous put-downs, name-calling, or other forms of abusive behavior.
- You have no place to go. Often friends and family are not helpful.
- You have feelings of powerlessness and fear.
- You believe that all you have in life is your family, house, children, husband, and/or marriage. They are your responsibility, and you must fix whatever goes wrong.
- You believe divorce is not a viable option.
- Your partner is not always abusive. After the violence, he is often contrite, asking for forgiveness, promising to change, and acting like the model father and husband . . . for a while.
- You feel trapped and do not know about support services.
- You believe that if you disclose the secret, no one will believe you. He is a pillar in the community and/or church.
- You believe the law will not take you seriously and that he will not be punished.
- You fear the complexities of the legal system. Lawyers are expensive.
- You still love him.

Appendix G

Reasons You May Leave an Abusive Relationship

- You believe the next abusive incident could be fatal.
- He is either sexually or physically abusing the children.
- The children are acting abusive, and you realize you need to remove them from the abusive situation.
- You are informed of available help via internet, radio, TV, church, etc.
- You are encouraged by other women who have left.
- You receive the support you need from a friend, family member, counselor, or church leader.
- You are learning to truly love yourself.

I find it interesting that the list of reasons to stay is nearly four times as long as the list of reasons to go. The more you attempt to justify staying, the longer your list will grow. Even more revealing, notice that nowhere in the reasons to stay does it mention loving yourself. As a matter of fact, if you carefully reread the reasons to stay, you will notice that each "reason" is fueled by fear, anxiety, faulty assumptions, and lies. But when it comes to needing a reason to leave, you truly need only one. Choosing to love yourself. And if you have children, loving yourself is loving them.

Appendix H

Why Abusers Don't Change

- Intrinsic satisfaction of power and control
- Ability to get his way
- Someone to take his problems out on
- Free labor from her, leisure and freedom for him
- Position as the center of attention
- Priority given to his needs
- Financial control
- Ensures that his career, education, goals are prioritized
- Status as partner and/or father
- Approval of friends/relatives
- Belief in double standards

Appendix I

Clear Signs an Abuser Has Changed

- Admits abuse toward current/past partners was unconditionally wrong
- Acknowledges his behavior was a choice, not a loss of control
- Recognizes the effects his abuse had on her and the children; shows empathy
- Identifies his pattern of controlling behaviors and entitled attitudes in detail
- Develops respectful behaviors/attitudes to replace abusive ones
- Replaces his distorted image of her with a positive, empathetic view
- Accepts the consequences of his abusive actions and commits to not repeat them
- Makes amends

- Accepts that overcoming abusiveness is likely a lifelong process
- Remains accountable for past and future actions

Appendix J

Clear Signs an Abuser Has Not Changed

- Says he can change only if she changes and "helps" him change
- Criticizes her for not realizing how much he's changed
- Criticizes her for considering him capable of behaving abusively even though he's done so in the past
- Reminds her of the bad things he would have done, but doesn't anymore, amounting to a subtle threat
- Tells her she's taking too long to make up her mind, pressuring her not to take the time she needs to assess his change
- Says he's changing, but she doesn't feel it

Appendix K

Biblical Perspectives on Abuse and Divorce

The sections below contain excerpts from several reliable sources. See the credit lines following each for more information.

The Biblical Option of Divorce

Often Malachi 2:16 is quoted as validation that divorce is not permissible: "'I hate divorce,' says the LORD God of Israel." But the entire verse says:

> "I hate divorce," says the LORD God of Israel, "and I hate a man's covering his wife with violence as well as with his garment," says the LORD Almighty. "So guard yourself in your spirit, and do not break faith."

When victims are told that the Lord hates divorce, they are most often not told that the same verse declares that God hates violence.

Why do we not tell victims and abusers that Proverb 6:17–19 lists seven things that the Lord hates: "haughty eyes, a lying tongue, and hands that shed innocent blood, a heart that devises wicked plans, feet that hurry to run to evil, a lying witness who testifies falsely, and one who sows discord in a family"? Why do we compel a victim to remain in a marriage characterized by these seven evils that the Lord hates? All too often the preservation of marriage has been exalted as the highest good, even when human life is at stake. This is not what the Bible says.

God's covenant with Israel was likened to a marriage union, one that was betrayed by an idolatrous wife. At three points in Scripture we are told that Yahweh has divorced His people (Isa. 50:1; 54:6–7; Jer. 3:8). Divorce was given not as a desirable option but as the least undesirable one in certain cases. The evangelical church cannot wholly condemn an action adopted by the Lord of heaven and earth in response to willful and persistent human sin.

The above material was taken from Catherine Clark Kroger and Nancy Nason-Clark, *No Place for Abuse: Biblical and Practical Resources to Counteract Domestic Violence* (Downers Grove, IL: InterVarsity press, 2001), chap. 12.

The Bible Does Allow Divorce for Domestic Abuse

One of the problems when dealing with domestic abuse in a Christian context is, "What does the Bible say about divorce for domestic abuse?" I believe the Bible allows divorce for domestic abuse, and the key text for this is 1 Corinthians 7:15: *"But if the unbeliever departs, let him depart; a brother or a sister is not under bondage in such cases. For God has called us to peace."* This verse has been generally assumed to relate to desertion: when an unbelieving spouse walks out, abandoning a marriage with a Christian spouse, but not legally divorcing them. However, in the Greek text the word depart (*chorizo*) means "to place space between, to separate," and it was one of the standard terms for legal divorce in the first century. Typically, perpetrators of abuse do not walk out of their marriages—they want to stay in the relationship because they enjoy the power, privilege, and control they obtain therein. So the victim of abuse thinks this verse does not apply to her. However, when correctly understood, it is the verse that gives her freedom.

In my book *Not Under Bondage: Biblical Divorce for Abuse, Adultery, and Desertion*, I define domestic abuse as a pattern of conduct by one spouse that is designed to obtain and maintain power and control over the other spouse. It always includes emotional and verbal abuse and may also include financial abuse, social abuse (restricting the victim's contact with family and friends), sexual abuse, physical violence, and spiritual abuse such as twisting scriptures to justify the abuse. Abusers who never use physical violence (and there are many) are still very frightening and controlling to their victims. Post-separation, many of these abuses may continue, with the added element of legal abuse leading to protective mothers sometimes losing custody of their children to the abuser.

The perpetration of domestic abuse effectively pushes away the other spouse and divides the marriage. The fact that many victims eventually leave abusive relationships testifies to this pushing away. Perpetrators usually protest that they want the marriage to continue, but their evil conduct conveys the exact opposite—it effectually pushes the opposite spouse away.

When applying 1 Corinthians 7:15, the key question is not "Who walked out?" but "Who caused the separation?" Would it be sensible to say that David was the sinful, rebellious one when he left Saul's court? No, he left because of Saul's abuse. David left, but Saul was the cause of his leaving. If we translate the word *chorizo* as "separate," we see this more clearly: if the unbeliever separates, let him separate. The unbeliever is doing the separating; the believer is commanded to let it be done. This tells the believing spouse (and the church) to allow the marriage to be over, because the unbeliever has destroyed the covenant. It permits the victim of abuse to take out a legal divorce. Let there be *chorizo* = let there be separation = let there be legal divorce, because the word *chorizo* means both separation and divorce.

In *Not Under Bondage*, I also show that since the brother or sister is not under bondage, the victim of abuse is free to remarry a new partner (unlike the instance in 1 Corinthians 7:10–11 where marriage to a new partner was forbidden).

The above material was taken from: http://www.restoredrelation ships.org/news/2016/01/11/domestic-abuse-divorce/. Guest blog by Barbara Roberts. Barbara leads the blog "A Cry For Justice," http://cryingoutforjustice.com/faq, which is seeking to awaken the evangelical church to domestic violence and abuse in its midst. Her book *Not Under Bondage* can be purchased at https://notunder bondage.com/ or at any book retailer.

What God Has Joined

Divorce is only allowed for a limited number of grounds that are found in the Old Testament and affirmed in the New Testament:

- *Adultery* (in Deuteronomy 24:1, affirmed by Jesus in Matthew 19)
- *Emotional and physical neglect* (in Exodus 21:10–11, affirmed by Paul in 1 Corinthians 7)
- *Abandonment and abuse* (included in neglect, as affirmed in 1 Corinthians 7)

Jewish couples listed these biblical grounds for divorce in their marriage vows. We reiterate them as love, honor, and keep and be faithful to each other. When these vows were broken, it threatened to break up the marriage. As in any broken contract, the wronged party had the right to say, "I forgive you; let's carry on" or, "I can't go on, because this marriage is broken."

Therefore, while divorce *should* never happen, God allows it (and subsequent remarriage) when your partner breaks the marriage vows.

The above material was taken from David Instone-Brewer, "What God Has Joined," *Christianity Today*, October 5, 2007, http://www.christianitytoday.com/ct/2007/october/20.26.html.

The Catholic Church Responds to Domestic Violence

Abused women often say, "I can't leave this relationship. The Bible says it would be wrong." Abusive men often say, "The Bible says my wife should be submissive to me." They take the biblical text and distort it to support their right to batter.

As bishops, we condemn the use of the Bible to support abusive behavior in any form. A correct reading of Scripture leads people to an understanding of the equal dignity of men and women and to relationships based on mutuality and love. Beginning with Genesis, Scripture teaches that women and men are created in God's image. Jesus himself always respected the human dignity of women. Pope John Paul II reminds us that "Christ's way of acting, the Gospel of his words and deeds, is a consistent protest against whatever offends the dignity of women."

Men who abuse often use Ephesians 5:22, taken out of context, to justify their behavior, but the passage (vv. 21–33) refers to the mutual submission of husband and wife out of love for Christ. Husbands should love their wives as they love their own body, as Christ loves the Church.

Men who batter also cite Scripture to insist that their victims forgive them (see, for example, Matthew 6:9–15). A victim then feels guilty if she cannot do so. Forgiveness, however, does not mean forgetting the abuse or pretending that it did not happen. Neither is possible. Forgiveness is not permission to repeat the abuse. Rather, forgiveness means that the victim decides to let go of the experience and move on with greater insight and conviction not to tolerate abuse of any kind again.

An abused woman may see her suffering as just punishment for a past deed for which she feels guilty. She may try to explain suffering by saying that it is "God's will" or "part of God's plan for my life" or "God's way of teaching me a lesson." This image of a harsh, cruel God runs contrary to the biblical image of a kind, merciful, and loving God. Jesus went out of his way to help suffering women. Think of the woman with the hemorrhage (Mark 5:25–34) or the woman caught in adultery (John 8:1–11). God promises to be present to us in our suffering, even when it is unjust.

Finally, we emphasize that no person is expected to stay in an abusive marriage. Some abused women believe that church teaching on the permanence of marriage requires them to stay in an abusive relationship. They may hesitate to seek a separation or divorce. They may fear that they cannot re-marry in the Church. Violence and abuse, not divorce, break up a marriage. We encourage abused persons who have divorced to investigate the possibility of seeking an annulment. An annulment, which determines that the marriage bond is not valid, can frequently open the door to healing.

The above material was taken from the United States Conference of Catholic Bishops, "When I Call for Help: A Pastoral Response to Domestic Violence Against Women," 2018, http://www.usccb .org/issues-and-action/marriage-and-family/marriage/domestic -violence/when-i-call-for-help.cfm.

Appendix L

Maneuvers an Abuser Uses to Keep You from Leaving

- Promises to change
- Enters therapy or an abusers' program
- Stops drinking/attends AA
- Apologizes
- Says no one else will want you
- Says you're abandoning him
- Threatens to kidnap/take custody of the children
- Threatens to withhold finances
- Acts nice
- Persuades others to pressure you into giving him another chance
- Threatens suicide
- Spreads rumors or your confidential information
- Starts a relationship/affair to upset you

- Insists he's changed
- Threatens or assaults anyone helping you or starting a relationship with you
- Gets you pregnant
- Stalks you
- Physically/sexually assaults you
- Destroys property
- Threatens to harm or kill you

Appendix M

Danger Signs an Abuser May Turn Violent When You Attempt to Leave

- Displays extreme jealousy
- Exhibits violent behavior and threats have escalated
- Monitors your whereabouts/stalks you
- Senses you're taking steps to leave
- Acts sexually violent toward you
- Threatens to kill/hurt you badly; chokes you
- Threatens you with a weapon; has access to them
- Is obsessed with you
- Acts depressed/suicidal
- Is a loner
- Has criminal history
- Acts violent toward you during pregnancy
- Abuses substances heavily

- Abuses the children
- Has been violent toward you or others in the past
- Kills/abuses pets
- Uses pornography
- Has acted violently during previous attempts to leave
- Is familiar with your routines and addresses of your friends, relatives, and workplace

Appendix N

Healthy Anger

- Healthy anger means observing and experiencing anger without being overwhelmed by it and reacting to it.
- Healthy anger means recognizing our anger as a signal to explore the feelings, thoughts, and bodily sensations that precede it.
- Healthy anger means viewing anger as a signal to direct our attention inward to identify our core desires, needs, and values.
- Healthy anger calls for developing self-compassion, which includes skills to enhance our sense of safety and connection.
- Healthy anger includes developing strategies to let go of anger, which may include forgiving others and ourselves.
- Healthy anger encompasses compassionate practices that don't cause suffering for others or for ourselves.
- Healthy anger means learning how to communicate assertively with others.
- Healthy anger enhances our resilience and overall well-being.

The above material was taken from Bernard Golden, "What Constitutes Healthy Anger," *Psychology Today*, August 17, 2016, https://www.psychologytoday.com/blog/overcoming-destructive-anger/201608/what-constitutes-healthy-anger.

Appendix O

Red Flags

Watch for the following red flags when you are considering an intimate relationship.

Physical Red Flags

- Flash of fear
- Sweating
- Tight stomach/tight jaw
- Pounding heart
- Hair standing up on the neck
- General feeling of discomfort

Spiritual Red Flags

- "Knowing" or "sensing" this isn't the person for you or the place for you to be in
- Knowing these things without any overt knowledge or concrete information

Mental and Emotional Red Flags

- From an emotional perspective, swinging wildly all over the place
- Friends telling you that you are different in a negative way
- Being more anxious than normal
- Feeling melancholy without knowing why
- Feeling confused about the relationship
- Feeling a general unease without knowing why
- Having difficulty sleeping, eating, or concentrating
- Abandoning normal activities for him or for the promise of him
- Having acquired some of his bad habits
- Thinking about things that are not reflective of reality

The above material was adapted from Sandra L. Brown, *How to Spot a Dangerous Man before You Get Involved* (Alameda, CA: Hunter House, Inc., 2005), 33–35.

Appendix P

Signs of a Bad Dating Choice

Signs of a bad dating choice include someone who:

- Doesn't respect your need for time alone
- Pushes to see you all the time
- Discourages your outside interests, family, and friends
- Asks you to do things you are uncomfortable doing (e.g., lying, lending him money, sex, etc.)
- Uses drugs (any kind of drug use should be a red flag)
- Uses alcohol too frequently and/or abundantly
- Is frequently unemployed (except while in school)
- Changes jobs frequently or is frequently fired or dismissed but always explains it away
- Wants to control your hair, dress, behavior, friends, job, or how you express your spirituality
- Wants you to quit or change jobs or friends for him
- Has had multiple unsuccessful relationships

- Has had any sexually transmitted diseases, currently or in the past
- Has a reputation for lying
- Conceals important information about himself that you only discover later
- Is physically, emotionally, verbally, or sexually "rough" or "weird"
- Is too charming, has all the right lines, comes across as excessively smooth

The above material was adapted from Sandra L. Brown, *How to Spot a Dangerous Man before You Get Involved* (Alameda, CA: Hunter House Inc., 2005), 205–6.

Appendix Q

Early Signs of Abuse

- Speaks disrespectfully about his former partners
- Is disrespectful
- Is controlling
- Does favors you don't want
- Is possessive
- Refuses to take blame for his actions
- Is self-centered
- Abuses drugs/alcohol
- Pressures you sexually
- Gets serious about the relationship too quickly
- Intimidates when angry
- Enforces double standards
- Displays negative attitudes toward women
- Treats you differently around others
- Is attracted to vulnerability

This above material contains excerpt(s) from WHY DOES HE DO THAT?: INSIDE THE MINDS OF ABUSIVE AND

Appendix R

Healthy versus Unhealthy Relationships

What Is Healthy?	What Is Unhealthy?
• Open and honest communication	• Game-playing and manipulative communication
• Having friends outside the relationship	• Having few friends outside the relationship
• Taking responsibility for the outcome of your life and happiness	• Making others responsible for your happiness
• Having your own identity	• Feeling complete only when involved with someone else
• A balance of time together and time apart	• Too much time together or too much time alone
• Emotional intimacy that is built without drugs or alcohol	• Use of alcohol or drugs to achieve false connection

What Is Healthy?	What Is Unhealthy?
• Appropriate level of commitment in the relationship	• Over- or under-commitment (based on the length of the relationship so far)
• Flexibility in the relationship	• Rigidity in the relationship
• Knowing what you needs	• Being clueless as to what you need
• Asking for what you need	• Afraid to express what you need

The above material was taken from Sandra L. Brown, *How to Spot a Dangerous Man before You Get Involved* (Alameda, CA: Hunter House Inc., 2005), 204.

Notes

Chapter 9 Do I Stay or Do I Go?

1. "Domestic Violence FAQs," Family and Child Abuse Prevention Center, 2005, http://fcapc.org/fcapc/faqs/index.asp?subject=dv.

2. "Is Change Possible in an Abuser?" The National Domestic Violence Hotline, September 5, 2013, http://www.thehotline.org/2013/09/05/is-change-possible-in-an-abuser/.

3. "Abuser Education," Emerge, 2013, http://www.emergedv.com/.

4. Lundy Bancroft, *Why Does He Do That? Inside the Minds of Angry and Controlling Men* (New York: Berkley Books, 2002) 339–342.

5. Bancroft, *Why Does He Do That*, 350–351.

6. United States Conference of Catholic Bishops, "When I Call for Help: A Pastoral Response to Domestic Violence Against Women," 2018, http://www.usccb.org/issues-and-action/marriage-and-family/marriage/domestic-violence/when-i-call-for-help.cfm.

7. Bancroft, *Why Does He Do That*, 213–214.

Chapter 11 Forgiveness Frees . . . You!

1. Anne Lamott, *Traveling Mercies: Some Thoughts on Faith* (New York: Anchor Books, 1999), 134.

Appendix C Hotlines and Resources

1. "About RAINN: RAINN's Mission," RAINN, 2018, www.rainn.org.

Acknowledgments

To Angela—You have stood by me with a quiet strength and an impenetrable faith that have withstood the darkest of days. You always held on to hope knowing someday I would be free. You never faltered. Thank you for believing for me until I could believe for myself. Thank you for letting me lean on you when I could not stand. You prayed me through this valley of weeping and wept with me when I hid my tears from the world. You are my Forever Friend to the grave and beyond. I love you.

To my Sweetie, Tim—I never realized that one of the greatest gifts I would receive from my decision to heal well was you. Not a day goes by that I don't thank God for bringing you into my life. You put the word *gentle* back into gentleman for me. You are not only a safe person but also a safe place where I continue to heal and grow into the woman God always desired for me to be. Thank you for encouraging me and praying with me throughout this entire writing journey. I am honored to be your wife. Thank you for believing in me. You are my beautiful husband, and I love you.

To my parents, John and Shirley—Your strength and commitment to family have carried me through some very painful and tumultuous trials. Thank you both for believing my life could be different. Thank you, Dad, for all of our wonderful talks on the back patio. Your wisdom is your legacy. Your steady reminder, "Prayer, perseverance, and perspiration," is what kept me going. Thank you, Mom, for truly being the "I-beam" in our family! Your love and strength of character uphold us all and have inspired me to pursue the best version of myself—free, whole, and with moxie back in my step. I love you both!

To my brothers, John and Dominic—Thank you, John, for being able to make me laugh when no one else could. Thank you for asking how my book was going when I hadn't yet written a single word. Thank you, Dom, for being direct yet loving with me. Thank you for exercising the courage to ask me, "What's happened to your moxie?" Today I walk and live with my moxie back. You had the guts to ask me when most were still pretending. Love you both!

To April and Lynnie—Because of you, I know the simple yet inconceivable love of Jesus. You two exemplify the heart of God in how you live and how you love. Thank you for taking me under your wings when mine were broken. You taught me how to mount on the wings of eagles and fly with Jesus! No fear. No dread. I love you both.

To Sandy—I believe God brings some people into our lives for a reason, some for a season, and some for a lifetime. He brought you into my life for all three. I am eternally grateful for your loyalty, your friendship, and your heart. My life is better because of you. Love you dearly!

To Erin—I have met very few people who have a heart as tender as yours. I will always cherish our long talks sitting on a park bench or a random street curb. When friendship is authentic, it doesn't matter where your life may take you because you're knitted together at the heart. Your love for Jesus transcends all you do. His love, being demonstrated through you, carried me in ways you may never know. Thank you for that gift. Love you, dear friend.

To Dr. Ken Nichols—You are my respected mentor, my encourager, my voice of reason, my friend. You have walked many years with me through peaks and deep valleys. Thank you for always seeing me beyond what I could see myself. You truly live a life worth emulating.

To Jessica Yaffa—Thank you for your emphatic declaration, "You gotta write this book!" as we had lunch together several years ago. You have my deepest respect as an overcomer yourself and one who has blazed the healing well and living free path for so many. Your organization, No Silence No Violence, is a wonderful resource for victims of domestic violence. You are incredible!

To my clients (both past and present)—Your lives and your stories have impacted my life in ways you may never know. Thank you for allowing me to sojourn with you as you have courageously chosen to pursue a better life. Some of my greatest lessons have come from you. I will always believe in you.

To each of you who has graciously permitted me to share parts of your story—Thank you. This book is not my story but our story. Abuse and the ripple effect it has in our lives connect us in a way that needs no words. You each are an overcomer. I am humbled and honored that you have entrusted me with the gift of your story.

To my faithful Wednesday morning praying warriors—Ladies, you are truly salt of the earth. Your prayers pierce heaven because your hearts embrace Jesus. I have felt the hug of your prayers throughout this journey. There is no way I would have completed this book without you. Because of your faithfulness, I am confident that this message will reach the hands of the least likely. Releasing captives. Setting prisoners free. Thank you all and please keep praying!

To my counselors, Dr. Martha Thorson; Raymond Cameron, MFT; and Dr. David Ferreira—Martha, you taught me to call it what it is . . . abuse. Raymond, you helped me grow a backbone and say, "Enough!" David, you gingerly and lovingly walked with me down the path of forgiveness and surrender. There are no words to capture my appreciation for your counsel and love. Thank you.

To my literary agent, Bruce Barbour, affectionately known as BRB—You saw something in me long before I saw it in myself. Thank you for recognizing the value of sharing my story and connecting me with a publisher who would do so. Your integrity, professionalism, and knowledge of the publishing industry truly made my writing experience a pleasure. I am humbled and incredibly grateful to have partnered with you, a stalwart and highly respected figure in the publishing world. Thank you, BRB!

To my editor, Jamie Janosz—You were instrumental in getting this writing project off the ground and did an incredible job of helping me to interweave my story throughout each chapter. The synergy between us fostered a momentum at the beginning that gave me the confidence that I could ultimately cross the finish line. Thank you, Jamie.

To my substantive editor, Ami McConnell—You were a master at setting me at ease as we worked together. Your editorial talent helped me integrate personal experiences with clinical expertise in a very fluid manner. You gave me the personal attention I needed in order to bring this project to a higher level. While I knew you had other authors you were working with, I always sensed I was a priority and that you genuinely cared about communicating my story in an authentic and sensitive manner. Your professionalism, patience, and prayer brought the very best out of me as an author. Above all, I am most appreciative for the sisterly kinship we developed along the way. God has no wasted moves! Thank you, Ami.

To my executive editor, Lonnie Hull DuPont—You saw the value of communicating this message and advocated on my behalf. Hence the reason this book was published. Without your vision of what this book could be, it would have remained with me alone. Your insights and editorial expertise were precisely what I needed to complete this project with excellence. Thank you for having a genuine and compassionate heart for this issue as well as the fortitude to bring it to fruition. Because of you, many victims of domestic violence will have the opportunity to heal well and live free. Thank you, Lonnie.

To my Revell team—Erin Bartels, Karen Campbell, Mackenzie Gibor, Jane Klein, Adam Lorenz, Jennifer Nutter, Erin Smith, Robin Turici, Cheryl Van Andel, and the entire Revell family—Your professionalism and personal support exceeded my expectations. Thank you for being an integral part of carrying this message to those who need to hear it. You have been a true pleasure to work with and a profound blessing to me personally.

Dr. Ramona Probasco holds a Doctorate in Psychology and has conducted extensive research in the area of domestic violence. She is a Marriage and Family Therapist, a Certified Domestic Violence Counselor, and a Nationally Certified Counselor. She has been in private practice for over twenty years. Dr. Probasco is an expert and sought-after speaker on domestic violence and how to authentically heal well from the trauma it causes. As a personal overcomer of domestic violence, she offers guidance and insight to others based on both her clinical expertise and her own experience of moving from victim to survivor to overcomer. She is an avid traveler, and some of her favorite places include Italy, Hawaii, and Jackson Hole, where she has hiked the forty-eight-mile Teton Crest Trail. She has also tried her hand at skydiving, scuba diving, and hot air ballooning. She is the mother of three incredible adult children and two wonderful adult children through remarriage, and she now thoroughly enjoys being the wife of a husband who absolutely adores her!